More praise for *Driving Results Through Social Networks*

"This book delivers on its promise by showing how leaders can fuel performance and growth through better management of networks within and between organizations. Cross and Thomas use in-depth case examples to move beyond the hype of networks and demonstrate the strategic benefits that come from leveraging these traditionally hidden assets. Having used these ideas in my own organization, I strongly recommend this book as a guide for leaders aspiring to obtain a multiplier effect on the skills and expertise of employees throughout a company."

John Cammack, *head of Third Party Distribution,*
T. Rowe Price Associates

"Informal networks are how work really gets done. While they are likely your most precious resource, most executives don't know how to harness their power. Cross and Thomas describe how to use them to meet your strategic objectives."

Steve D'Amico, *director of Design Learning and Capability,*
The Procter & Gamble Company

"People-centered managers have intuitively believed that improving connections at work result in significant quantifiable business impacts. Cross and Thomas now give us proof that this intuition is true! At MWH, we've used organizational network analysis inside our company and with our clients over the past five years to successfully manage organizational design, improve leadership and mentoring, facilitate change, and improve knowledge retention—we're believers. If you want to be a believer, let this book give you new insights and starting points for using this important, new approach to business management."

Vic Gulas, *chief knowledge officer,*
Montgomery-Watson Harza

"While individual know-how is critically important for our company, it is network-based knowledge and connections that drive our ability to act and operate globally, driving better business performance. Our best networks continuously analyze how they are actually functioning, enabling these networks to improve collaborative patterns and produce greater business value. This book breaks new ground in highlighting concrete connections between networks and business performance."

Dan Ranta, director of Knowledge Sharing,
ConocoPhillips

"Better networks mean better performance. That's never been clear before this book, but now it's obvious. If you know your business objectives, Cross and Thomas will help you understand how social networks can help you achieve them."

Thomas H. Davenport, President's Distinguished
Professor of Management and Information Technology,
Babson College

"Organizational network analysis has become an indispensable way of thinking and framing knowledge sharing within the Defense Intelligence Agency and the Intelligence Community. We have used it to baseline the level of leadership collaboration, to implement a "smart mentoring" concept to pull up those at the periphery of frontline employees to be more influential with peers and leaders, and to show that greater diversity of one's network is directly correlated with higher performance. We have taken from Cross and Thomas more than they have given—a performance improvement capability that is changing the landscape of organizations."

Adrian (Zeke) Wolfberg, director, Knowledge Laboratory,
Defense Intelligence Agency

Driving Results Through Social Networks

How Top Organizations Leverage Networks for Performance and Growth

Rob Cross and Robert J. Thomas

JOSSEY-BASS
A Wiley Imprint
www.josseybass.com

Published by Jossey-Bass
A Wiley Imprint
989 Market Street, San Francisco, CA 94103-1741—www.josseybass.com

Jossey-Bass books and products are available through most bookstores. To contact Jossey-Bass directly call our Customer Care Department within the U.S. at 800-956-7739, outside the U.S. at 317-572-3986, or fax 317-572-4002.

Jossey-Bass also publishes its books in a variety of electronic formats. Some content that appears in print may not be available in electronic books.

Library of Congress Cataloging-in-Publication Data

Cross, Robert L., 1967-
    Driving results through social networks : how top organizations leverage networks for performance and growth / Rob Cross and Robert J. Thomas.
        p.   cm.
    Includes bibliographical references and index.
    ISBN 978-0-470-39249-2 (cloth)
        1. Business networks. 2. Social networks. 3. Management. I. Thomas, Robert J. (Robert Joseph), 1952- II. Title.
    HD69.S8C757 2008
    658'.044—dc22

                                                        2008036104

Printed in the United States of America
first edition
HB Printing   10 9 8 7 6 5 4 3 2 1

The Jossey-Bass

Business & Management Series

Contents

Preface

Most leaders readily acknowledge the importance and power of informal networks for getting work done in their organizations. Yet they generally spend little if any time assessing and managing these networks—a mistake with substantial implications for innovation and performance. Network analysis provides a powerful means for leaders to understand and drive value through this seemingly invisible aspect of organizations. Does information flow smoothly across formal structures and allow the organization to leverage scale and expertise in product or service offerings? Is innovation spurred at key points by effective networks that knit together functions, offerings, and technical capabilities? Is the organization overly focused on a few decision makers, roles, or experts who are invisibly but dramatically slowing the work and efficiency of many others? Once networks become visible, leaders can address these and other questions in ways that have immediate impacts on performance.

Of course, network analysis is not new by any stretch. The approach has enjoyed a rich research tradition within anthropology, sociology, psychology, and management studies.[1] A vast body of knowledge on techniques for the analysis of social networks has been accumulated, dating back to Dr. J. L. Moreno's attempts in the early 1930s to map all of the relationships within New York City.[2] In fact, the analytic side of the social network discipline has become so rich that one of the most widely read primers on social network analysis is more than eight hundred pages long.[3]

Yet although network analytics have advanced substantially over the past decades, the managerial applications of the ideas have not kept pace. This comparative lack of attention to business applications led Rob Cross to publish a book in 2004 on managerial uses of network analysis within organizations, as well as software to improve leadership effectiveness (a free preview of this application can be found at www.robcross. org). The ideas from this book, *The Hidden Power of Social Networks*, resonated with a wide range of organizations and led to the formation of a consortium called The Network Roundtable (http://www.thenetworkroundtable.org) to further explore business applications of network analysis. The Network Roundtable grew rapidly to include ninety influential and well-known companies and government agencies. Yet rather than develop another tool or diagnostic to apply to their organizations, members of the consortium asked that the research focus instead on specific ways that network analysis could help leaders identify improvement opportunities that cannot be unearthed with current frameworks (such as formal structure) or diagnostics (such as process maps, culture surveys, and employee engagement inventories). A daunting challenge issued by a tough, smart, and demanding set of leaders! But one that was unquestionably worth pursuing in close collaboration with these organizations.

The Network Roundtable was consequently organized to accomplish two important goals. The first goal was to teach members how to apply network analysis to critical business issues. Online tutorials, hands-on workshops, webinars, and accessible training materials were provided to enable members to undertake a range of projects in their own organizations. This resulted in a stream of innovations on the application of network analysis to key business issues as members with varied backgrounds and interests took up the ideas in their own ways—an important process that often broke us free from existing paradigms of thought on network analysis.

The second goal of The Network Roundtable was to support a series of research programs that yielded *actionable insights* and *measurable business impact*. Over a five-year period these programs have focused on ways that network analysis can improve: (1) Innovation and Top-Line Revenue Growth, (2) Client Connectivity and Sales Force Effectiveness, (3) Large-Scale Change and Post-Merger Integration, (4) Talent Management and Leadership Development, (5) Strategy Execution and Alignment, (6) Financial Return Through Effective Collaboration, and (7) Lateral Connectivity in Organizations (such as Best-Practice Transfer). In each of these programs we worked with Roundtable members to understand the business results that leaders can attain through targeted improvement to networks.

In comparison to more traditional, case-based research, this approach was a significant challenge. In business writing, an authors' main challenge often is locating a company or leader who is *already* doing something interesting and convincing that organization to conduct some interviews and share their success. In contrast, the path we went down was more consuming. For our research to be successful, we had to (1) convince a leader to allow us to come in and conduct a network analysis on a group of strategic importance; (2) administer a sometimes lengthy survey and produce a detailed analysis with compelling and actionable insights; (3) convince the organization to invest time and sometimes money in making changes based on the network insights we provided; and (4) conduct a follow-up network analysis six to nine months later to assess strategic, operational, and financial impact. Only then—sometimes as long as two years after we started conversations with an organization—could we begin interviews and document examples in which network analysis yielded *actionable insights* and *measurable business impact*.

As you can imagine, this was a complex undertaking that was made possible only by the generous and inquisitive spirit of many Network Roundtable members. Working through this process with a wide range of organizations—for five or six years in some cases—has enabled us to develop a unique set of insights into ways that network analysis can be used as a strategic tool to generate value in organizations.

We hope to make two contributions toward that end with this book. First, we describe a series of critical business issues for which network analysis provides unique means to leaders for improving their organizations. Rather than suggest simply applying network analysis to any group in an organization, we offer readers a set of applications that have consistently yielded substantial business impacts in our research. Second we have accumulated a broad range of cases that draw specific links between network analysis insights, actions taken on the basis of those insights, and concurrent improvements to business performance. We are aware of no other base of experience that is more substantial in pinpointing business results derived from network analyses within organizations. This book offers stories of success based on repeatable processes you can use in your own organizations to recreate this performance impact. Although the stories and network insights will be different in your organization, the results you can derive by focusing on critical but often invisible networks have proven out repeatedly.

A network perspective, as we show in the upcoming chapters, provides principles and tools with which to fashion collaborations that reduce complexity, increase speed to market, and multiply the impact of key talent. Through vivid examples drawn from leading organizations, we show how a network perspective can dramatically enhance performance in three areas vital to survival and success in a connected world: *alignment, execution,* and *adaptation.*[4]

Part One: Alignment shows how a network perspective helps leaders to identify points of misalignment and accelerate collaboration in the right places and at the right times. *Part Two: Execution* uses network analysis to help leaders determine whether targeted units or functions are achieving the kind of connectivity necessary to produce desired results, and if they are not, how to identify and track surgical interventions. *Part Three: Adaptation* shows how a network perspective can help organizations identify high performers, understand how they use their networks to maximum effect, and replicate the behaviors and relationships that make them successful.

In the book's concluding chapter, we offer some provocative thoughts about the future of organizations as seen through a network lens. One day leaders will be able to dispense with confusing (and perennially out-of-date) organization charts and diagrams and replace them with imagery—network movies—that accurately portray the dynamism of a living system in real time. We hope you enjoy reading this book as much as we have enjoyed writing it!

Acknowledgments

This work is a product of a rich and vibrant network. Collaborations and conversations with various scholars have honed our thinking on the strategic benefits that a network perspective provides to leaders. Close work with leaders in a wide range of organizations applying these ideas has continually pushed us to use network analysis not simply as an interesting concept, but as a tool for generating actionable insights and measurable business value. Both kinds of interaction have been central to our research, and it is to these myriad relationships that this book is dedicated.

It is impossible in a short acknowledgement to give credit to all the people who helped advance our thinking. Almost every page in the book was informed by someone who provided an important insight. We assure all who worked with us that your contributions are truly appreciated, and to each person we express a heartfelt thank-you!

Two institutions require recognition. First, we thank the McIntire School of Commerce at the University of Virginia for enabling the consortium (The Network Roundtable) through which so many of these ideas have been tested and developed in the past four years. We are extremely appreciative of the leadership at McIntire—Carl Zeithaml, Ellen Whitener, Gerry Starsia, Adelaide King, and Tom Bateman—for helping to create such a rich forum and giving Rob the time to pursue these ideas. Of course we also want to express a sincere thank-you to the corporate and government sponsors of The Network Roundtable.

Their willingness to explore network ideas in their own organizations has resulted in the core of this book.

In addition, we wish to thank Accenture for providing the time and resources with which to test and refine the network approach. In particular, we greatly appreciate the foresight of Walt Shill, Tim Breene, and Ana Dutra, who recognized the possibilities in these ideas and made investments to ensure that the book was produced. In addition, we would like to thank several of the staff at Accenture's Institute for High Performance Business—Josh Bellin, Dave Light, and Elizabeth Craig—and consultants Carrie Newberry, Natalie Mich, and Lisa Finkelstein for their thoughtful contributions.

On the editorial front, we are extremely grateful to two people who helped bring this work to fruition. First, Kathe Sweeney carefully guided us through the process with Jossey-Bass. She has provided invaluable guidance on this book from the framing of the work to detailed editorial suggestions. Second, this book is much improved owing to the constructive and tireless editing of Amy Halliday. Her contributions have been enormous in terms of both substance and style, and we are truly grateful for her time.

Finally, we thank our families. Your patience and support are the only means by which endeavors like this come to fruition!

Introduction

Anne Downing was an industry veteran recruited to lead a new but growing business unit at one of the world's largest professional services organizations. Although she was an experienced professional, Anne's challenges were stiff ones: she was new to the company, she was expected to achieve significant revenue growth in her first year, and the leader who preceded her had brought into the unit many people she did not know and who did not know one another.

Anne believed that rich networks were the key to revenue growth and effective management of employees in professional services, but she didn't have the luxury of time to meet everyone and get to know their strengths and weaknesses. Her concerns weren't just social; if the right people weren't collaborating in sales situations or delivering solutions to clients, revenue would suffer and she would never hit her ambitious growth targets. Moreover, she couldn't tell from quarterly reports alone who in her group was doing the best job of mentoring younger employees, working across organizational boundaries with industry groups, or devising new insights and perspectives with which to win future business. She was impatient to act, yet reluctant to make changes until she understood their potential impact.

To come up to speed as rapidly as possible, Anne asked us to conduct an organizational network analysis (ONA), which quickly gave her the range of insights she needed to improve performance and innovation in this global group. "What I found so helpful about the analysis was its specificity," she told us. "I had seen network diagrams before in presentations, but they had always been abstract—lines and arrows connecting people I did not know or need to worry about. It was an entirely different experience looking at my own group. The results jumped off the page with immediate opportunities."

The ONA confirmed Anne's fears that the people in her unit were only loosely connected. Against an ideal level of 30 to 40 percent connectivity (with 100 percent being complete connectivity and high inefficiency, and 0 percent being equivalent to a group of strangers), only 12 percent of the possible connections existed in her unit. This did not bode well for sales or service delivery. The analysis also revealed that the people most often sought out for information and support were not always the most senior employees. Some people were in central positions by virtue of their role (for instance, administrative staff responsible for scheduling people on assignments); others were in central network positions because, despite their lower status, they were up-and-coming talent. What was surprising was that several people who were revealed as most critical to substantial project sales were not formally recognized as high revenue generators by the firm's accounting practices.

Upon viewing the ONA results, Anne started to make changes and get key people connected. She encouraged central players to bring those network members they weren't familiar with into client meetings and proposal development efforts. She reached out to people on the periphery of the network who were known for their creativity and new ideas and invited them to share their expertise in weekly staff meetings and ongoing service development efforts. And she implemented new criteria in performance reviews to track each individual's support of client sales and project execution in other industry groups.

The ONA also gave Anne insights into two truly powerful categories of people: revenue generators and time savers. She discovered, for example, that the ten people who had been identified through the ONA as the most crucial collaborators on sales had supported efforts accounting for nearly 60 percent of the revenue generated in the preceding year, and the top five people accounted for 38 percent of the total. The loss of even a few of these people would be devastating, yet little was being done to secure their loyalty or to ensure that they were mentoring high-potential employees. Anne also discovered that the ten people revealed as having saved the most time of others in the unit by sharing key resources, information, and expertise had in fact saved time equivalent to half the unit's salary cost. In other words, a few people—many of whom were not high performers in revenue terms—were responsible for the lion's share of cost containment.

Eager to protect critical assets, Anne worked hard to get to know these top revenue generators and time savers. One-on-one conversations yielded important insights about their individual aspirations and motivations and afforded Anne a much clearer sense of what it would take to keep the people productive and satisfied. Equally important, she uncovered ways to connect these experts to people they did not know in the unit and to people in industry groups who had complementary expertise. These collaborations generated several new service offerings and helped integrate some experts who had become isolated. Further, Anne was able to enlist these highly valuable employees as mentors for newly hired staff, which bolstered the veterans' engagement with the practice while also helping to slingshot newcomers into the network.

Anne took the network results a step further to see who participated in the highest-value sales collaborations (greater than $2 million) and who participated in the lower-value collaborations (under $250,000). This view enabled her to take specific actions to encourage more profitable sales efforts. Not all prospective clients are equal; some represent significant revenue opportunities but low odds of a successful sale; others may not be as large in terms of potential revenue, but the probabilities of a successful sale are much higher. Through the ONA, Anne was able to identify clients and types of sales efforts that consumed the time of her unit but yielded the smallest margins. This information in turn enabled her to focus her group on high-probability sales, to raise the quality of work delivered, and to pursue follow-up sales through more creative combinations of expertise.

A year into her tenure as unit head, Anne credited the ONA with being a major contributor to the group's success. A second ONA revealed that the unit's overall connectivity was just over 40 percent—nearly a fourfold increase. Employee engagement scores had improved dramatically, billability had nearly doubled, and both revenue and margin targets had been met. Now more than just a descriptive tool, the ONA was a strategic weapon: "One look at the ONA results and I can tell where we are prepared to mobilize a team to address an opportunity and where we're probably not prepared. For me it provides powerful information—information I can share quickly and easily with my leadership team—that I cannot get anywhere else."

Many leaders are experiencing similar performance breakthroughs today. Organizational network analysis has emerged as a powerful new way for leaders to see what goes on inside their organizations, to diagnose problems and opportunities, and to stimulate innovation and performance. By quickly revealing hitherto invisible networks, ONA makes it possible for leaders to identify collaborative hot spots and cold spots in their organizations and to monitor critical points of value creation. Moreover, ONA lets leaders intervene where necessary—and only where necessary—to provide direction without interrupting normal operations.

In contrast to traditional approaches to organization design, which have relied almost entirely on formal structure, ONA gives leaders tools and principles with which to design and rapidly reconfigure networks to execute strategic objectives most effectively. Rather than pursuing strategic objectives through tightly drawn reporting relationships, incentive schemes, and performance management systems, the approach provides leaders with robust new methods for cultivating collaboration precisely where it is needed in measured and manageable ways. And instead of using highly regulated HR processes for recruiting, developing, and retaining talent, ONA helps leaders identify a network's high performers—the critical individuals who connect important constituencies—and outliers—the people whose influence or expertise may spell the difference between innovation and stagnation, success and failure.

Part One

ALIGNMENT

How to Ensure That Networks Support Strategic Objectives

In a 2006 article published in the *Financial Times*, business school professor Henry Mintzberg railed against the obsessive focus on individual leaders as the fulcrum of organizational effectiveness: "By focusing on the single person . . . leadership becomes part of the syndrome of individuality that is undermining organizations."[5] We agree, of course, but to be fair, the fixation on leaders as individual actors results from the lack of an alternative framework. We simply haven't had a different lens through which we could connect individual efforts and organizational action. Some have turned to elaborate formal structures as a means of connecting individual and organizational behaviors. But formal structures often overlook the fact that every formal organization has in its shadow an informal "invisible" organization. This informal organization, which is brought to light by organizational network analysis (ONA), need not be seen as opposed to the formal organization, but may instead be seen as an answer to the inevitable shortcomings of a formal structure.[6]

ONA provides leaders with the means to accomplish what is arguably their most critical function: aligning individual and collective action with strategic objectives. Leaders *are* individuals in a formal structure, but they are also embedded in networks that all too often do not show up on the organization chart. In addition to rendering the invisible visible, a network perspective helps leaders understand how much alignment they actually need. Alignment and collaboration require energy and attention, so indiscriminate efforts to foster collaboration can easily impose high costs on employees in terms of increased e-mail traffic, phone calls, meetings, and travel. Decision makers can become so overwhelmed that they cannot act on commercial opportunities, and entire organizations can get bogged down. For these reasons, leaders need to take a strategic view of exactly what they want to accomplish through networks and then ensure that formal and informal aspects of an organization support critical collaborations.

In Part One, we show how leaders can actively diagnose and align networks with core value propositions and strategic objectives—a process of both increasing collaboration at key points of value creation within a network and decreasing connectivity where it is generating insufficient financial or strategic return.

1

ALIGNING NETWORKS
WITH STRATEGIC VALUE
PROPOSITIONS

Every day you have conversations at work with peers whose opinions you respect and whose friendships you value. It is likely that you report to a superior whom you also like and respect but often do not see for days and sometimes weeks at a time. Both interactions have impact, but the first conversation is "invisible" on most organization charts. Formal structure determines in large part who is sought out in networks: we are driven to reach out to people by virtue of the decisions they get to make, the information they hold, and the resources they dole out. But informal relationships are crucial as well: some people may lack formal authority but possess technical expertise and organizational wisdom, or they may simply be likable and dependable and so an important source of help and information.

Although these networks of both formal and informal relationships are increasingly the conduits through which value is created and innovation realized, most leaders still rely too heavily on formal structure when designing their organizations and implementing strategy. The process of moving boxes and lines around on a formal chart can make leaders *feel* as though they are driving alignment and organizational focus on strategic objectives, but in fact these formal changes often do not shift the underlying networks. The result is a disconnect between strategic objectives and network configuration that leads organizations to underperform relative to the expertise and resources they possess, or to create unmanageable collaborative demands with efforts that indiscriminately connect people. When, however, leaders employ a network perspective, they can ensure that collaborations deep within the organization are supporting strategic objectives as efficiently as possible.

Consider the story of a $1 billion provider of information technology consulting services with ten thousand employees spread across more than seventy offices globally. In late 2005 the company launched a strategic initiative to move from a branch-and region-centric structure to a matrix organization with globally integrated business lines and vertical consulting practices working in conjunction with a regionally based sales force. The strategic reason for this change was to better focus the company on clients while also increasing scalability, reducing costs, accelerating growth, and improving career opportunities. Management had an aggressive timeline for the transformation, expecting the majority of the restructuring to be completed by mid-2006 and to be fully operational by the end of the year.

To establish a baseline of the firm's ability to work across boundaries, the senior vice president of human resources conducted an ONA of the top 250 executives and managers. The assessment, which mapped both information flow and revenue-producing collaborations, revealed a number of ways in which this network was potentially misaligned with the strategic intent of the new matrix organization. For example, the information flow network revealed that employees relied heavily on senior leaders. Those lower in the hierarchy—who had critical expertise and key relationships with clients—tended to be on the outer rings of the network and so were not bringing the best expertise of the firm to bear on client sales and project execution. These people were often the single point of contact with key accounts, and they typically had a substantial—but to this point unrecognized—impact on revenue when they left the firm.

The ONA also revealed that several silos in the network were likely to undercut the organization's ability to realize benefits from the new matrix structure. For example, most collaboration occurred first within a region and then within a business unit. A select set of silos became a focal point for the restructuring, with the goal of ensuring that employees transcended formal structure in cross-selling and in delivering holistic solutions that could differentiate the organization in the marketplace. Beyond information flow, the ONA also made it clear that the top 250 executives were not aware of the skills and expertise available through the network that could be leveraged in client work. Raising awareness at key points in the network became a critical precursor to increasing revenue-generating collaborations, bringing the best expertise to client projects, and boosting productivity through best-practice transfers.

While the company took a range of actions to align the network with strategic objectives, special attention was paid to leaders who the ONA revealed were overly central. That is, the ten most sought-out people in the network—all but one of whom were in the top ranks of the organization—had from twenty-four to fifty-one people coming to them frequently for information. This network imbalance made it hard for many employees to gain access to these leaders. Through no fault of their own, the leaders had become bottlenecks, causing delays in decision making and slowing down projects and sales efforts. They also represented substantial susceptibilities in the network in that removing just these ten people (less than 5 percent of the top three layers in the organization) decreased the number of revenue-producing collaborations in the network by 26 percent.

Clearly, the excessive demands made on this small set of leaders needed to be reduced in order for the organization to succeed in the new matrix structure. As a result, the company initiated four specific actions. First, the chief information officer implemented an expertise locator to help people find resources across the organization and established global solution teams so that subject-matter experts were leveraged across regional boundaries. Second, the chief financial officer redefined dollar thresholds so that pricing decisions could be made by lower-level employees. For instance, a team one level below the vice presidents was given decision rights regarding solutions and pricing, a move that dramatically reduced the time and effort it took to approve relatively small, low-risk projects. Third, educational sessions were held on such topics as service offerings, delivery experience for service offerings, and rules of engagement between regions and business lines in order to facilitate understanding across the organization about how to work in the new matrix structure (see Figure 1.1). Finally, the senior team worked to develop a culture of responsiveness and increased information flow down and across the hierarchy by encouraging people to return calls and e-mails within twenty-four hours regardless of the seeker's title or position.

Although the firm took care to alleviate some of the relational demands on those at higher levels, it also realized that these highly connected leaders, given their influence, could help drive change. For example, as the leader of the newly formed Application Services unit, one of the largest global groups, Peggy Smith was well connected. Yet even within her own group's network, she saw that people were not collaborating across regions. Instead of creating committees among those in certain positions within the formal structure—a common approach to repairing such collaboration problems—Peggy used the ONA results to identify highly connected people in various regions and then forged ties among them. This helped Peggy and her direct reports to rapidly and efficiently build awareness across regional boundaries of who knew what.

A second ONA, conducted six months later, showed that the network had become much more closely aligned with the strategic

Figure 1.1. Facilitating a Matrix Structure Through Targeted Connectivity

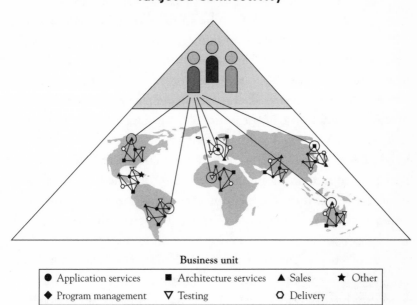

Business unit

● Application services	■ Architecture services	▲ Sales ★ Other
◆ Program management	▽ Testing	○ Delivery

objectives set out for the matrix structure. First, collaboration was more evenly distributed and employees were able to get information they needed and decisions approved much more rapidly. Second, the group as a whole was getting greater leverage from its peripheral members, many of whom were in key client-facing roles. For example, the second ONA revealed a 17 percent increase in ties to and from account managers who had previously been on the network's periphery. Not surprisingly, these new relationships had had a positive impact on client-service and account-penetration measures. Third, the network was now better integrated across functions and regions, an improvement crucial to the success of the matrix structure (see Figure 1.1). Specifically, employee collaborations across functions had increased by 13 percent and resulted in numerous examples of improved client service, sales, and best-practice transfer at these junctures.

In sum, ONA accelerated the company's transformation from a branch-centric to a global operation. One highly central vice president indicated that "the ONA was helpful in realizing why we lacked nimbleness and quick turnaround times for RFPs or unsolicited proposals. Creating points of contact and information conduits across business lines and regions helped us assemble teams with needed skills, knowledge, and experience more efficiently, enabling faster time to market." Results from the second ONA showed a 27 percent increase in sales collaborations of up to $500,000, a 15 percent increase in sales between $500,000 and $2 million, and a 9 percent increase in client sales between $2 million and $10 million. In aggregate, these results boosted the firm's revenue by nearly 10 percent on an annualized basis.

What made this transition such a success was that leaders attended to both informal and formal structure. The network analysis played a crucial role in helping leaders—such as Peggy—build bridges much more rapidly to well-connected experts throughout the global organization. Equally important, it helped the organization see what would happen if key account managers left, and how to get better leverage out of high-end experts who had drifted to the fringe of the network.

But these and other changes to the network would be only temporary if not accompanied by changes to formal structure. Annual planning processes, project start-up practices, human resource processes, and technology—to name just a few—were all aspects of the formal organization that were shifted to create a context in which the right collaborations were more likely to occur and flourish over time. In this instance, the appropriate aspects of formal structure to consider were those that helped in the transition to a more client-centric, matrix-based structure. In other organizations—for example, those that thrive on process excellence and efficiency—very different structural elements must be in place to promote the right network configuration.

Network Archetypes and Value Propositions

Networks enable organizations to do two things: recognize opportunities and challenges, and coordinate appropriate responses. But the kind of network an organization needs in order to be most effective and efficient will depend on its value proposition, its strategic objectives, and the nature of its work. Through our work in a wide range of industries, we have identified two network archetypes that characterize the two ends of the spectrum: the customized response network and the routine response network. These two kinds of networks are each suited for a specific value proposition and demand certain investments.

> *Customized response networks.* These networks develop in order to define a problem or an opportunity rapidly and coordinate relevant expertise in response. They are "custom" in that the value of these networks derives from both the framing of a problem and the creation of an innovative resolution. Organizations obtaining value from customized response networks include strategy consulting firms, high-end investment banks, new-product development consultancies, and early-stage drug development.

> *Routine response networks.* These networks operate best in environments where both problems and solutions are fairly well defined and predictable, and the work is standardized. Value is delivered through efficient and consistent responses to established problem domains. Insurance claims processing, call centers, and late-stage drug development, for instance, all require low-cost and reliable coordination of expertise to solve commonly occurring problems.

In Table 1.1 we have outlined both salient network characteristics and organizational decisions that must be made to support each kind of network. We now turn to case descriptions of both archetypes.

Table 1.1. Designing Value-Based Networks

	Customized Response	*Routine Response*
Context	Solving Ambiguous Problems	Solving Established Problems
	Unknown Problem	Known Problem
	Unknown Response	Known Response
Value Proposition	Rapid definition of problem or opportunity space and coordination of relevant expertise to solve problem. Value is delivered both in the framing and then in the innovative resolution of the problem space.	Low-cost and reliable coordination of relevant expertise to solve routine or known problems. Value is delivered through efficient and consistent response to a set of established problem domains.
Network Features		
Connectivity		
Internal	Dense and redundant connectivity within and across boundaries	Connectivity focused on process flow of defined problem
External	Diverse external connectivity to sense opportunities and respond	Limited and targeted external connectivity
Formal structure	Formal structure plays minimal role in dictating collaboration	Formal structure focuses collaboration on inputs and outputs
Relational capital	(1) trust in others' expertise, (2) generalized reciprocity	(1) trust in process execution, (2) accountability to perform role
Locating experts	Ability to identify dispersed expertise quickly	Predefined by process flow
Strategic Decisions		
Pricing	Premium pricing allows reinvestment in social capital	Commodity pricing

	Customized Response	Routine Response
Structure	Permeable boundaries (inside and outside); decentralized decision rights and information access	Defined internal and external boundaries; defined and embedded decision rights and information access
Work management	Planning focuses on general markets and expertise; controls focus on output rather than coordination	Planning focuses on offerings; controls focus on efficiency and reliability of delivery
HR practices	Hire, develop, and reward T-shaped skills and collaborative behaviors	Hire, develop, and reward for specific task execution
Technology	Expertise locators and portals	Work-management systems and artificial intelligence
Culture and leadership	Collaborative within and across organizational lines, norms of generalized reciprocity	Centralized decision making, focused on standardization and task accountability
Examples	High-end investment banks, consulting firms, corporate R&D, early-stage drug development	Insurance claims processing, call centers, late-stage drug development

Customized Response Case Study: Novartis

Novartis, a Swiss pharmaceutical company, won Federal Drug Administration approval in May 2001 for Gleevec, a breakthrough medication that arrests a life-threatening form of blood cancer, chronic myeloid leukemia (CML). Gleevec, a tiny orange capsule, enjoyed the fastest approval ever granted by the FDA for a cancer drug and is considered revolutionary because of the way it treats CML. Traditional cancer therapies combat the disease through surgery or a combination of toxic drugs and radiation that destroy cancer cells as well as some normal cells. As a result, often patients are left feeling extremely weak and suffering from severe side effects. Gleevec is the first cancer drug that targets a cancer-producing molecule and fixes the genetic malfunction without harming healthy cells. "Our hope is to turn cancer into a chronic but treatable disease," says Alex Matter, formerly head of Oncology Research at Novartis, who discovered the drug with his team of scientists.

Gleevec is the product of a customized response network. Alex Matter and his team challenged the traditional treatment of CML and created something new based on cutting-edge developments in gene therapy and the selective targeting of cancer-producing cells. The breakthrough drug that resulted from their efforts required what Dan Vasella, CEO of Novartis, described as *innovation management*—calling on a wide variety of internal and external expertise to define and solve the problem, challenging assumptions by engaging scientists across disciplines, and taking creative risks in both drug discovery and delivery.

The networks that created Gleevec were nowhere apparent on Novartis's formal organization chart—in fact, diverse connections external to Novartis were altogether pivotal to the success of Gleevec. Before Novartis even existed, Matter worked at Ciba-Geigy in Switzerland and had been considering ways that kinases, or enzymes, might affect cancer growth by inhibiting cell proliferation. At the time, no one was pursuing the idea of inhibiting kinases as a type of treatment—most scientists thought it would be impossible.

But Matter persisted in seeking out scientists who could point the way to diseases that his team might target. He relied heavily on his external contacts—including Brian Druker and Tom Roberts at the Dana Farber Cancer Institute in Boston—to keep abreast of cutting-edge ideas in fields relevant to cancer treatment. Druker, a medical oncologist, knew that CML was the most promising cancer for research using the approach that Matter was contemplating. It was the only cancer in which the genetic cause had been scientifically established. Druker's research interests overlapped with Matter's and provided fertile territory for exploring a new way to treat cancer. Later, when Matter and his team were at Novartis and had discovered and tested in animal trials a compound effective against CML, external connections became critical in identifying the hospitals where the first patients would receive the drug in trials.

Extensive internal connections at Novartis were also critical at each stage of the drug development process. Effective internal networks—which crossed the boundaries of traditionally distinct scientific disciplines such as chemistry and biology—allowed fertile brainstorming in drug development. Similarly, other internal collaborations were critical to manufacturing success. Once the drug was approved, the company undertook a new manufacturing approach. Rather than making small quantities of the new drug in the Basel, Switzerland, plant and then moving to the company's sites in Ireland for mass production, Novartis decided to move directly from technical development to one of the Ireland sites—a change that shaved a year off the normal production schedule. Dense and trusted networks across geographic boundaries were essential to this approach.

Of course, the networks that led to the production of Gleevec didn't develop overnight. Many Novartis executives questioned the unusual and high-risk approach. Crucial to the success of Matter's team, however, was the unwavering support of the CEO. Vasella trusted Matter's competence and judgment and gave him both the freedom and the political support to develop a new approach to cancer treatment and coordinate the right network of collaborators. He also helped this global network rise to the challenge of cutting a year off the normal production schedule and accelerating FDA approval by rearranging priorities within Novartis. Vasella's trust was well placed: one day after the drug won approval from the FDA, it was ready to ship. Gleevec was available in retail pharmacies three days later.

Customized Response: Success Factors

The network characteristics that enabled Matter and his team to define a novel approach to a complex problem and assemble the right expertise to develop an innovative solution did not arise on their own. Management made strategic decisions that enabled such a network to develop. Novartis's organizational structure was deliberately designed to allow internal and external boundaries to be crossed. As Matter points out, "We bring together different disciplines, functions, and geographies to try to break up silos." The global oncology business unit reaches across different geographies in their marketing, sales, and research functions. Novartis also has decision boards that cross technologies and facilitate collaboration between groups that are often segregated in other companies.

Novartis takes a markedly different approach in their planning processes as well, pushing executives to consider ways that the unique packaging of expertise—both within and outside the organization—could help the company create and respond to market opportunities. The organization forms alliances with industry partners and academic institutions to develop products, acquire platform technologies, and access new markets. Its Disease Area Strategy, which focuses on alliances and acquisitions for key disease areas and on indicators expected to be growth drivers for Novartis, is but one example.

This collaborative environment is also supported by carefully considered leadership and human resource practices. Managers are encouraged to take risks and to help younger scientists reach out to colleagues with unique expertise in order to consider breakthrough innovations. In the course of developing Gleevec, Matter was at the hub of a network that connected Novartis employees with researchers, administrators, and patients in medical establishments throughout the world.

Core to Novartis's success is their ability to produce while still encouraging experimentation. When we wrote this case study, Novartis had seventy-eight projects in clinical development or registration, had received seven major approvals for drugs during 2003, and had launched eleven new medicines in the United States since 2000. This high productivity helped to engender collaboration. Novartis's pharmaceutical products pipeline is among one of the broadest in the industry, and employees are encouraged to reach out and respond to requests for help through both formal and informal mechanisms such as team awards and public recognition for the successful screening of compounds.

Finally, Novartis invests in technology, such as globally validated databases, to help manage the vast sea of knowledge relevant to research and commercial functions, creating a privileged knowledge environment for its scientists. In keeping with its commitment to create a collaborative and productive environment, Novartis recently announced plans to convert its headquarters in Basel from an industrial complex to a facility that emphasizes innovation and provides employees and visitors with an environment of intensive levels of communication and work. The new campus will have buildings with open designs and meeting places that encourage spontaneous exchanges.

In January 2004, *Fortune* magazine voted Novartis one of the top ten European companies to work for—the only health care company on the list. Employees value the collaborative nature of the organization and the networks that individuals form and come to rely on across hierarchical, geographic, and organizational boundaries. As the Gleevec success highlights, effective networks in companies such as Novartis deliver value by framing and then solving problems in new ways, which is essential to innovation in a highly competitive market. Creating a context that supports this kind of work requires appropriate investments in infrastructure, organizational design, and leadership.

Routine Response Case Study: Sallie Mae

Sallie Mae, America's leading provider of education loans, owns or manages approximately $100 billion in student loans for more than seven million borrowers. Deborah Bragg, who runs the call center, states the organization's mission: "Our goal is to resolve a customer's question on the first contact while minimizing service expense to the company." This is no small task. With nearly seven million calls each year, Deborah and her team must make sense of an enormous jumble of calls and questions from customers, a process that requires both formal and informal collaborations. Internal connections must focus on creating process flows that can work across a variety of requests, such as questions about a new product. Whereas at Novartis internal connections need to be dense, spontaneous, and boundary spanning, Sallie Mae requires a more efficient network defined by process flows.

The call center's management team consistently identifies changes in customer input to address problems so that the output is improved customer service. For example, repeat-call trends (customers who have to call multiple times to have their problems solved) are analyzed at least monthly to identify reasons for higher volume. If the reason has to do with another part of the company, internal feedback is provided. Or if a new loan product is unclear to customers, a system is in place to alert the group responsible for the new product. As Deborah explains, "Focused collaboration allows us to deliver clearer information to our customers and, in turn, reduces repeat and additional calls, improves customer service, and contains costs."

Process flows help define whom to go to for internal expertise. The center has an interdepartmental referral process which ensures that call center agents can quickly direct customers to the appropriate person and department. So if, for example, a parent who already has a loan through Sallie Mae calls the center because he or she needs a loan for another child, the call center agent can quickly direct the call to the person who handles new loan approvals. And if an individual agent doesn't have expertise in the caller's area, Sallie Mae has a call-escalation process in which an agent refers a call up a hierarchy of specialists who have more experience, usually longer tenure, and more decision-making authority.

At the same time, process flow must be balanced with good customer service—what Deborah Bragg calls *nimble servicing*—to prevent the network from taking over and becoming both too consuming and more ad hoc. To this end, Sallie Mae uses a process called *hot topics,* in which agents write an online summary of recurring issues, provide examples, and apply e-mail management so the issue can be assigned for review and resolution. Once a resolution is determined, the topic is turned into a Knowledge Tool, a user-friendly, online resource available to agents in real time. After typing in a key word based on a caller's question, an inexperienced agent receives a document with all the information he or she needs—information that represents the call center's collective experience and expertise.

Routine Response: Success Factors

Deborah Bragg and her colleague Debra Walsh have made several strategic decisions related to structure, work management processes, human resource practices, and technology to support the efficient coordination of expertise and reduce the need for expensive, unproductive interactions in the call center network. In short, they have facilitated the development of network patterns consistent with the call center's core value proposition of consistency and efficiency in handling customer inquiries. The operation's structure is designed to incorporate expertise into the processes, tools, and technologies with well-defined internal and external boundaries.

For example, Sallie Mae uses work management processes that emphasize the reliable delivery of service to customers through approaches such as coaching for best practices, calibration exercises, and peer review. Calibration exercises are designed to identify issues that will lead to better outcomes. Every week, supervisors, trainers, and quality assurance staff review and score agents' calls. They discuss variances, identify gray areas, and develop best practices. These practices are then used to enhance training and update the Knowledge Tool. Management also continually evaluates the call escalation process to see which agents are escalating the most calls (and therefore might need help or more training) and whether the specialists are able to respond. All of these approaches continually and systematically help to keep work from creeping into the network and resulting in inefficiencies and inconsistent responses across agents.

Call centers have also installed human resource practices that emphasize hiring, training, and rewarding agents for superior service. These human resource practices are consistent with the company's leadership and culture, which emphasize accountability as one of the core values. Encouraging individual accountability for tasks helps facilitate a network that is highly focused on inputs and outputs and in which internal connectivity does not become overly dense. To improve service, Sallie Mae moved to performance-based scheduling, in which an agent's performance-based score is determined by the quality of his or her work, attendance, and productivity. "Those with higher scores have the option to work the more desirable shifts," Deborah explains, which provides incentives for performance. Compensation and career advancement are also tied to the performance-based score.

Sallie Mae fosters individual training for agents to help cultivate a sense of accountability. When agents begin working at Sallie Mae, they spend six weeks in a classroom setting learning basic tools and technologies and the quality assurance review process. These agents then focus on developing different skill sets, depending on the type of calls they will be handling. To complement classroom training, Debra Walsh, who is responsible for technical and "soft skills" training, deploys computer-based training to allow agents to learn new skills, such as how to handle a new repayment option, at their own pace. This approach avoids having to pull agents into the classroom and away from the customer. It also provides consistent training among the call center's three sites and gives agents immediate feedback on their individual skill development. The program is flexible, agents like it, and it saved Sallie Mae more than $300,000 in its first year.

Finally, Sallie Mae employs several technologies to help agents obtain the expertise they need without reaching into the network. The Knowledge Tool is one example. Managers also use a quality-monitoring system that allows them to hear and evaluate agents' performance. And to better serve the customer, Sallie Mae has updated its web-payment service, allowing for smaller call-center volume and happier customers. In this case the hot topics forum revealed that the service on this site was not as user friendly as it could be, resulting in more calls from customers. Deborah's management team worked with a cross-functional group within the organization responsible for the site to deploy a more robust product. Within three months, call-center volume for issues related to bill payment fell more than 75 percent, from more than twenty thousand to less than five thousand calls per month.

By maintaining and continually updating the routine response network, Sallie Mae avoids the inefficiencies of a large, dense network. According to an independent research firm that benchmarks the average score for the financial services industry at 74 percent, 88 percent of Sallie Mae customers were satisfied with their most recent calls to the center. Embedding information and knowledge in processes when work can be standardized has significant advantages. In a context like Sallie Mae's, this approach avoids the high transaction costs and service-inconsistency issues that arise when each employee must find someone who can help answer customers' questions. "We want no error, no issue that would impair our customer service mission to go undetected," Deborah says, "and for us that means targeted collaboration."

Conclusion

Work and innovation are inherently collaborative endeavors, but as the need for collaboration increases, the demands on people's time skyrocket. The answer is not more and more layers of a matrix structure or yet another collaborative technology.

Rather, what's required is a more nuanced and strategic view of collaboration on the part of leaders as designers of their organization. Instead of mandating collaboration or assuming that more connectivity is better, leaders need to focus on the core network components that will deliver value and on the few high-leverage organizational design variables that will support these networks. They need to recognize that networks take different forms and require different support depending on the goals of a given business unit or of an entire organization.

This chapter has shown leaders how to determine which network characteristics can deliver on specific value propositions and what investments in formal structure will help nurture appropriate connectivity. Four steps are important in this process:

1. Define the core value proposition of a network either as a product of how it supports strategic objectives of the organization or through that network's ability to enable the organization to sense and respond to key market opportunities and threats.

2. Identify the critical relationships that must exist for the network to support strategic objectives. These relationships will always be unique and depend on strategic goals, but the dimensions discussed in this chapter provide a guide to the key network categories that leaders should always consider.

3. Conduct an organizational network analysis to assess existing collaborations and alignment between the current network and the ideal network needed to support strategic objectives. Comparing the current and ideal network defines targeted investments that leaders must make to both de-layer points where excess connectivity is reducing efficiency and build collaborations at targeted junctures where integration of expertise can improve performance or innovation.

4. Put in place an organizational context—using the design elements presented in Table 1.1—that enables the right networks to flourish and develop over time. Although leaders rarely have the ability to influence all aspects of organizational design, often they do have the latitude to modify four to five dimensions that, if not corrected, will drive networks back into unproductive tendencies.

2

WORKING THROUGH NETWORKS TO ALIGN CULTURE AND STRATEGY

Virgin Group chairman and founder Richard Branson acknowledges the importance of aligning business strategy and culture with his organization's ability to diversify and grow, yet remain cohesive: "Our culture is who we are and our culture shapes how we do business. You don't stay in business and propagate new ventures the way we do without making sure that cultural values and business practices are in tune with one another." Indeed, some companies find that managing corporate culture so that it meshes with strategic objectives can lead to better performance. Harrah's Entertainment, a Las Vegas–based casino and hotel empire, actively instills and reinforces a performance culture among its employees, to the point of analyzing, measuring, and providing feedback on individual behaviors. According to Harrah's director of customer service, "We have discovered that an upbeat, positive attitude is the most important attribute to our customers. . . . We know how to describe what it looks and sounds like, and we train to it. We certify observers to measure it, we score it in real time, and we give employees ongoing feedback."[7]

Yet although most leaders pursue cultural alignment, success is elusive and there are myriad well-known cases of failure—such as the failed merger of German auto manufacturer Daimler-Benz and U.S.-based Chrysler, the spin-off of upstart beverage company Snapple from consumer products mainstay Quaker Oats, and the slow integration of dozens of separate agencies into the U.S. Department of Homeland Security.[8] One of the biggest challenges that leaders face stems from the fact that they lack a lens through which to view how culture operates, and they lack the tools to achieve greater alignment. Like leaders who simply shift boxes and lines on a formal chart and believe they are aligning the organization with its strategic objectives, those who use broad cultural change programs to align culture with new initiatives are too often disappointed with the results. ONA provides an incredible advantage by allowing leaders to see how culture is distributed throughout a network, whether beliefs and values are integrating in a way that supports strategic objectives, or whether diverging values, practices, and goals are invisibly but inevitably tearing the organization apart.

In the face of dwindling market share, the computer division of one of the world's largest consumer electronics organizations was under the gun to improve product development speed and quality. To innovate rapidly, engineers with disparate expertise and varying positions in the formal hierarchy were told to collaborate. Mechanical and electrical engineers were to come together to design lightweight, thin, power-efficient notebook computers for a fast-growing segment of the market; and software developers were to work closely with electrical engineers to create the hardware's multimedia components. Unfortunately, these collaborations didn't happen, which resulted in frequent decision-making delays and the inability to innovate quickly enough to gain a foothold in this market.

To help accelerate innovation, we conducted an ONA of this division's top 105 engineers and managers, using both a cultural inventory and a network survey focused on collaboration. The cultural inventory gave us a sense of the employees' values and attitudes on a number of important dimensions, and the network analysis allowed us to see the relative prominence of those values and attitudes in the network. From the network

Figure 2.1. Hierarchical Levels of Employees in a Consumer Products Electronics Firm

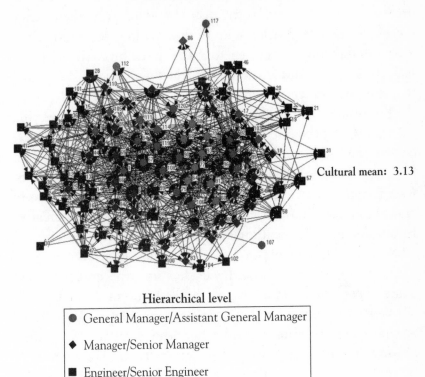

Cultural mean: 3.13

Hierarchical level

● General Manager/Assistant General Manager

◆ Manager/Senior Manager

■ Engineer/Senior Engineer

assessment alone we learned that information flow had become very hierarchical. The lines in Figure 2.1 illustrate who turned to whom for work-related information, and the shapes of each node (person) in the network reflect hierarchical level. In general people were seeking information from those above them in the hierarchy; engineers, who are on the periphery of the network, were not being consulted as frequently as senior managers, who are central. In addition, information silos existed across departments and projects as well as between headquarters and an offsite manufacturing facility.

In short, the network assessment confirmed management's suspicions that ineffective collaboration undercut the organization's ability to innovate and thereby maintain, much less gain, market share. Unfortunately, the division's leaders weren't sure what was driving these disconnects or what could be done about them. They suggested possible problems in work-flow and decision-making processes that forced engineers to reach up the hierarchy for information. It was by using the ONA, however, that we discovered that the real problem lay with employees' cultural beliefs.

Essentially, the leaders and the engineers were operating according to different norms and values. The engineers perceived the culture as rigid; upper management believed it to be highly flexible.[9] This finding was eye-opening to the leaders, who felt they had created an adaptive organization and were crafting market and product strategies that anticipated creativity and lateral collaboration, yet the engineers' actions reflected a belief that the organization did not value initiative and innovative thinking. Somehow the leaders and the engineers had come to operate according to very different norms and values.

What accounted for these opposing perspectives? The leaders' perspectives were shaped when the company was growing rapidly and competition was not so fierce. The engineers, however, experienced day-to-day work life under a great deal of pressure and found their creative latitude hindered by tight deadlines and the need for myriad sign-offs on critical decisions. As a result, the engineers had little time for collaboration or exploration of ideas outside of immediate project goals.

The ONA also uncovered cultural value gaps among the engineers themselves. For example, the assessment revealed that employees cared about different things in their work and that this in turn was dramatically fragmenting the network. Certain engineers focused heavily on usability in product features while others were principally concerned with style and portability. These different values were never explicitly recognized in any meetings and therefore silently led to project delays due to competing perspectives. Cultural perceptions among the engineers also varied on the basis of their work responsibilities. Engineers who worked on multiple projects (for instance, both notebook and desktop computers) were generally more positive about the culture and had a big-picture view of the organization and a broader network to tap for information and resources. In contrast, project managers—a critical role in the organization—tended to remain on a single project and were influential in the network, but were often negative about the organization's culture because they felt overly burdened.

The leaders of this division knew that breakdowns in collaboration were hindering innovation; however, they had difficulty determining what was wrong and how to fix it. Together the ONA and the culture assessment gave them the ability to see how formal structure, such as hierarchy and role, and cultural values were leading to breakdowns in information flow, problem solving, and decision making. As a result, they instituted a number of new practices, such as leadership development and interpersonal coaching, revised staffing and rotation programs, new project-planning and budgeting processes, and project management practices that encouraged reaching out into the network at crucial points in a project. These efforts were highly targeted—and ultimately extremely successful—because they helped the leaders understand precisely where and how to exert influence in the network that would yield the greatest short- and long-term success.

Driving Results Through an Integrated View of Culture and Networks

Culture and employee engagement or satisfaction surveys can be analyzed to show differences in attitudes and beliefs in organizations. For example, these surveys can reveal if employees are more positive in certain functions than in others or if leaders feel differently about the culture than followers. Along a range of dimensions—such as demographics, position in formal structure, and tenure—responses to culture questionnaires can be averaged by various subgroups and then compared to help leaders see where they should target their efforts.

Although interesting, these views of culture provide little insight into the networks that make certain voices and perspectives more important than others. They do not allow leaders to see, for example, which values are held by those who are highly central in the network and therefore more influential in the organization. The remainder of this chapter shows how combining culture surveys with ONA can help leaders drive alignment in three ways: by working through key culture carriers, by correcting cultural fragmentation in networks, and by identifying values that have become overly dominant.

Working Through Key Culture Carriers

We assessed a well-known government agency with a network of people distributed across a range of intelligence gathering and analysis functions. This agency employs more than 7,500 military and civilian employees worldwide. It produces and manages foreign military intelligence to inform combat troops, defense policymakers, and force planners, and to support U.S. military planning, operations, and weapon systems acquisition. A typical project involves intra-agency or interagency collaboration, sometimes on a large scale, in an attempt to include all relevant sources of knowledge.

The pilot network we assessed had been formed to promote more effective cross-functional integration in data collection and analysis. We were asked to determine how effective this network was in breaking through traditional silos and becoming a model of lateral collaboration for the agency. These outcomes were critically important to the agency because traditional approaches to collecting and interpreting tactical information were not sufficient for dealing with increasingly sophisticated threats (such as biological, chemical, and nuclear weapons) coming from diverse national contexts (such as North Korea and the Middle East). These new threats demanded new ways of acquiring intelligence and making decisions, and as a result the agency was investing substantially in technology and physical space reorganizations that could help employees with different expertise collaborate and respond to threats with a holistic solution.

At the group's inception, a network analysis revealed that although the network was somewhat connected in terms of information sharing, some members (generally those who had been in the agency the longest) were overly central, while many newcomers were stuck on the periphery. The network was also fragmented by both directorate (the agency's equivalent of a business unit) and physical location, which hampered the agency's ability to synthesize information regarding the technical, political, and cultural dimensions of threats. These problems were exacerbated by enduring features of the organization's culture. Cold War veterans, for instance, clung to ways of looking at the world that were not necessarily shared or even understood by younger employees.

Here we combined the Cultural Values Inventory with a fairly typical ONA.[10] Together these assessments provided a rich view of what highly influential employees saw as the agency's current cultural values and of what they thought those values should be. We were also able to identify the key culture carriers by overlaying the network information on the results from the culture inventory.

It turned out that the most central people in the network were both positive and negative culture carriers. As one example, people who believed that the organization *was* flexible and learning oriented and those who believed it *was not* flexible and learning oriented were the most influential in the network. In this seemingly odd scenario, which in fact is very common, the actions of positive and negative culture carriers canceled each other out. For instance, when the more energized and passionate people started to build momentum around an idea, equally influential people who believed things could not be improved or that new ways of working were not sustainable squelched their efforts.

The ability to visualize these culture carriers and their influence on the network creates substantial opportunities to drive cultural change. Negative culture carriers who are highly central are prime candidates for behavioral coaching, developmental staffing efforts, and even mentoring relationships that allow them to pass on what they know and so derive a greater sense of worth and purpose from their work. Quite often we have found that when leaders simply pay a little extra attention, they can have a dramatic impact on the attitudes and actions of the negative culture carriers. These people often have quite a bit to contribute but have become disaffected. Although leaders can't court every person in the organization, we have found that finding and working with the top five to ten such players in a network can have dramatic effects that then spread to others.

In a similar way, leaders can reinforce the behaviors of positive culture carriers by celebrating and rewarding their actions, and they can encourage these behaviors systemwide by embedding them in performance assessments. Engaging these influential positive voices in change processes also helps leaders shift a culture because they have the right people on the design teams who then become ambassadors for the effort. Paradoxically, leaders must also make sure that these people do not unintentionally become bottlenecks. Too often these central players can have a substantial impact on a transformation effort but become overloaded as longtime colleagues continue to come to them for information along with new colleagues who have been thrust upon them through a restructuring. These highly skilled and effective—but overloaded—people burn themselves out and introduce substantial inefficiencies if plans are not put in place to help them manage their personal connectivity.

To avoid this scenario, the leaders organized an offsite meeting with well-connected members of the network to discuss opportunities to promote more effective interagency collaboration.

The first portion of the meeting covered the network analysis results; the second focused on teaching storytelling techniques as a way to drive cultural change through the network.[11] Leaders have long known that the best way to communicate and mobilize commitment to a course of action is to present ideas in an engaging narrative. What they have struggled with is how best to spread these stories throughout their organizations—a process that ONA and cultural inventories can greatly help by identifying positive cultural carriers who are influential in the network. In the workshop, success and vision stories were crafted to be communicated by the positive culture carriers to the broader network as a first step in shifting cultural values and old work practices. These stories varied, but all contained examples of instances when cross-agency collaboration had yielded important results.

Another low-effort, high-impact initiative the agency undertook, Smart Mentoring, came from leveraging the network's centrally positioned culture carriers to integrate peripheral experts and bridge key points of network fragmentation. Specifically, the agency established a structured mentoring program to help brokers—those who sit between functions—and peripheral employees connect in ways that had value for both. Influential brokers exist in all organizations, but often go unrecognized because they are not highly visible in any given subgroup and are frequently not in a position of formal authority. But because they are not immersed in the day-to-day interactions of any one group, brokers appreciate the expertise and values of other functions or subgroups in the network and so have a unique ability to contribute to network and cultural alignment.[12]

Susan, a mentee who had recently started working in the agency's Human Capital department, quickly realized that as a new employee she needed to establish relationships with employees across directorates as quickly as possible. The results from the first ONA, however, indicated that only three people went to her for information on a regular basis. Having received this wake-up call, Susan began to reach out to brokers and central people in subpockets throughout the agency. A second ONA conducted nine months later showed that nineteen people sought her frequently for information, with fifteen of them spread across functional groups outside of the Human Capital department.

Another mentee, Joan, had been at the agency for a year but had an inadequate understanding of how things worked. Joan was given a mentor, Mary, who was able to provide her with a sense of organizational structure, an understanding of how everyone's job fit into the organization, and insight into some of the tacit cultural norms. Over time this mentoring relationship helped Joan see how to execute her role most effectively in the context of the agency's mission, as well as how best to navigate the power structure and informal networks. The relationship was also beneficial for Mary, giving her a morale boost as she passed on her experience.

Through fairly simple but targeted actions, our ONA and culture analysis yielded very positive results. An assessment conducted one year later revealed a significant improvement in information flow (a 24 percent increase in helpful relationships). Although the peripheral people's information-seeking networks had grown, most interesting was that the number of people tapping these newcomers' expertise had tripled—an increase due in no small part to the introductions they had received from their well-placed mentors. The second assessment also revealed a significant improvement in culture: there had been an 18 percent increase in the culture scores, indicating that both employees and leaders felt the organization was becoming more decentralized and flexible. The gap between the perceived and desired work environment had also shrunk substantially, and 235 new collaborative relationships had each generated substantial value through, for instance, best-practice transfers and innovative means of integrating intelligence across the agency.

Addressing Cultural Drivers of Network Fragmentation

Network analysis also allows us to see the extreme positions held within networks that can undermine organizational effectiveness but remain invisible in standard culture assessments. Survey-based assessments of culture often characterize norms, values, and assumptions by averaging survey responses.[13] For example, suppose you asked employees to rate an organization on a dimension such as openness, meritocracy, or ethical decision making using a five-point scale on which 1 is "strongly disagree" and 5 is "strongly agree." You find that you have two extreme clusters in a network—one that strongly agrees that a value exists and therefore rates it an average of 5, and another that feels ambivalent and so rates it 3—scores that cancel each other out, producing an average response of 4. Without the benefit of the network analysis, the leader who sees this average calculation may just accept it, unaware of the very different cultural experiences of the two subgroups. She would be in the unfortunate position of believing that things were better than they were.

ONA is a critical tool in addressing rifts in culture. It lets leaders see exactly how culture is distributed and where gaps undermine performance. Consider the research and development function of a global pharmaceutical firm that was the product of a merger between U.S. and European parent companies. The managers were keenly aware that cross-cultural problems could arise, and they knew that the decision to standardize many laboratory procedures, in particular, could expose some cultural divides. Almost a year into the merger integration effort, management conducted an ONA to measure progress in integrating the R&D unit. Initial results were promising: although there were three discernible national subgroups, there appeared to be strong communication among them.

The picture became more nuanced, however, when leaders also focused on certain cultural practices. To reveal gaps in culture, we first conducted a series of interviews to identify norms and practices and then used the results to create questions that we included in the network analysis. A typical question was, "(True or False) Clinicians become involved in project teams early in the development process." In combination with the ONA results, the answers to these cultural-practice questions revealed that although there was consensus on some matters, many important practices had not diffused well in the network.

Consider, for example, management's widespread efforts to standardize the assays that scientists used to determine a compound's properties. The network analysis revealed that well-connected scientists in each of the subgroups agreed that standardization *had not* taken hold, while senior managers and team leaders in each location felt that it *had*. The senior managers and leaders were the ones who were wrong—they simply had too little day-to-day interaction with the scientists to be aware of the varying practices. Instead, they were making decisions and crafting strategic plans on the basis of a wide range of beliefs that turned out to be far from the truth.

A note of caution here: It can be highly misleading to tell a manager, on the basis of a network analysis or culture assessment alone, that two groups that need to work together are doing just fine. Employed individually, each assessment may show satisfactory levels of communication or shared values even when specific barriers to successful collaboration persist and drive inefficiencies. Only by combining network and cultural views on a range of issues could the leaders begin to ensure consistency and realize the benefits from the merger.

ONA is also useful in helping to isolate misalignment with strategic objectives that is driven by differing values and assumptions even when organization design and leadership decisions have been made that should result in an aligned organization. It is often only after looking more closely at ONA results that leaders are able to locate subcultures and silos created by differences in what people care about in their work. For example, in one merged company, we found a difference in the perceived value of outputs. One product-development group focused on features and style while the other had a history of concern for safety. We encountered similar circumstances in a major alliance between a well-known pharmaceutical company that was progressive in thought and practice and an established consumer-products organization that was highly controlling and conservative. Similarly, in a merger of two consulting firms, hidden conflicts emerged over legacy values: One firm focused on maintaining long-standing client relationships and the other focused on more immediate sales and profitability.

In these and other cases, organization design and leadership decisions had been made that should have resulted in an aligned organization. It was only after looking more closely at ONA results that leaders were able to locate subcultures and silos created by differences in what people cared about in their work. Such differences are typically output oriented (such as a focus on product style rather than safety) or process oriented (such as flexible versus structured approaches to work). Yet too often, instead of being recognized as divergent perspectives to be explored and bridged, the differences are used by one group to label the other: "they are too rigid" or "they are not reliable." Combining cultural values with ONA enables a leader to achieve a more complete view of how different values and practices are causing network breakdowns.

Identifying Dominant Beliefs and Values

In many cases, trouble arises not because views differ but because beliefs or assumptions become so pervasive that they reinforce negative patterns of interaction and restrict new ways of working.[14] Sometimes the assumptions are obvious and can be articulated, such as flexible versus inflexible work styles. Other times they are subtle and operate tacitly, dictating how people spend their time or what they care about in their work. In such instances, ONA can be helpful in unearthing hidden but influential assumptions so they don't inflict more damage.

Managers at another large pharmaceutical company learned this the hard way. The organization was in the midst of an initiative to consolidate operations and obtain benefits of scale in R&D. Business units were spread across three continents, separate functions were involved in the consolidation effort, and there were some residual rifts between legacy units from a prior merger. Midway through the consolidation process, management paused to analyze the networks developing in various units. There were some concerns, but in general it appeared that fairly robust cross-unit ties were forming. Moreover, the culture assessment suggested that employees in general saw the organization as task focused and structured, and as having clear direction, goals, and objectives. The picture seemed positive, but in practice the subunits had not been able to execute projects that required integration among the old functional areas. Furthermore, political struggles over resources had begun to emerge.

At this point we began a series of interviews with employees from a range of functions. All interviewees acknowledged the challenges of restructuring, but most expressed a genuine interest in finding projects on which to collaborate with their new colleagues. We then asked, "What is the key strategic priority for this new unit right now?" One after another, interviewees began to give different answers: "Building our own skill set and knowledge base," "Speeding up R&D's overall development cycle," and "Adopting uniform technical standards." In the end we had a list of eighteen "top" priorities. Thinking that we had somehow been leading interviewees in our discussions, when we conducted the ONA survey we asked everyone in the unit to identify in rank order the top five priorities from the list of eighteen possibilities. In this case, twelve of the eighteen options received at least one first-place vote. Clearly, although unit members had a consistent, overarching belief that things were going well and that no substantial problems existed with collaboration across the networks, our ONA showed that they were tearing themselves apart in the pursuit of conflicting objectives.

Based on the top twelve priorities identified, we found there were two overarching sets of priorities. On the one hand, there were "marketing" concerns: enhancing the unit's product range and understanding internal client needs. On the other hand, there were "technical" priorities: improving specific applications and unifying technical standards. People who gave high ratings to marketing priorities tended to come from the same legacy company and tended to give low ratings to technical priorities, and vice versa.

Having such large numbers of employees subscribe to sharply different priorities was clearly a concern. It also appeared to be a self-reinforcing loop. The organization's dominant values— which were shaped by a Germanic cultural background and long-held organizational norms—contributed to a sense that people should respect bureaucratic boundaries. This meant that the widely shared agreement that the unit's culture was task-focused and structured, which managers had originally lauded as a sign of growing consensus, actually reinforced the idea that those pursuing one set of priorities had no need to consult with those pursuing the other set. In short, the fact that employees agreed so strongly on the importance of divisional boundaries meant they had no basis for agreeing on priorities.

The ONA helped identify a range of simple but effective interventions. First, the leaders organized a series of meetings to share these findings and then agree on new goals and priorities. In these meetings, the network analysis helped catalyze the need for change and resulted in a wide range of almost comical stories about people's efforts canceling each other out despite the best intentions. To determine the unit's direction, the leaders presented what they called the ideal project. This mythical project enabled the leaders to show how the various skills and abilities of this new group could be integrated on key efforts in powerful ways. The dialogue that emerged from the initial discussion of the ideal project, and subsequent discussions on impediments to achieving such a project, quickly helped inform new ways of working together.

Management also learned the importance of articulating their objectives and leveraging their influential players to craft both a strategic and an operational way of working together. Taking the time to identify the specific cultural elements that were impeding the change effort kept managers from undertaking an overly ambitious program of change. Staffing highly influential people in each subgroup on key projects and important internal committees helped bring the prior organizations together quickly and thus further eased the transition. In general, the more fine-grained managers' assessments of the dominant cultural paradigm in an organization are, the more precisely they can work to change relevant norms and values.

Conclusion

Alignment is critical to organizational effectiveness. It's also a core leadership responsibility. Former GE and Goldman Sachs executive Steve Kerr put it nicely: "Anybody can create divisions; integration is the hard part." Alignment and integration require a great deal more than formal organization charts and value statements. To understand the dynamics that promote integration and collaboration, leaders need a clear view of how cultural forces shape and in turn are shaped by the interactions that constitute an organization's network structure. In this chapter we have demonstrated ways in which networks and culture can work together to sustain—or undermine—organizational change. Whether the context is a restructuring, a merger, or merely the ongoing improvement of a business unit, successful interventions rest on an awareness of cultural values and assumptions as they are distributed across networks.

Ironically, this awareness rarely derives from intuition or from a general feel for the organization. Time and again we have found leaders' instincts about organizational culture to be highly unreliable. It is too easy to convince ourselves that the culture we experience as individuals through our immediate network interactions must be the culture of the organization as a whole, or to fall into the leadership trap of imagining that formal organizational structures and values statements are stronger than they actually are. It is also too easy to underutilize central players who embody the desired cultural values and can play a key role in teaching others to collaborate, and it is all too easy to ignore brokers who have developed broad-based outlooks that can help reconcile subcultures.

The approach we have described in this chapter can supplement leaders' intuition and systematically create collaborative and adaptable organizations. Four steps can help generate greater cultural alignment:

1. Define the cultural values, goals, and practices that are critical to alignment with strategic objectives. Once articulated, these can be measured along with an organizational network analysis, thereby enabling leaders to improve cultural alignment by reshaping networks.

2. Identify the positive and negative culture carriers that are central—and therefore highly influential—in the network. Both positive and negative culture carriers frequently occupy central network positions and thus cancel out each others' efforts. Once these carriers are identified, however, leaders can work uniquely with each category of employee to help break this gridlock.

3. Specify key points of network fragmentation between cultural values and goals. Far too often, networks that should otherwise be aligned on the basis of formal structure continue to work at cross-purposes because employees

care about and pursue different objectives. Seeing these competing forces in a network enables much more targeted means of aligning goals than methodologies focused on formal structure alone.

4. Locate dominant values situated in a network in positions that preclude a group from adapting new ways of working. Often these values are held not by those high in the hierarchy, but rather by seemingly invisible people at key points in the network—important players whose impact is made visible and actionable only when viewed through a network analysis.

Next, in Part Two, we demonstrate how a network lens improves the execution of three core processes in organizations: innovation and coordination through lateral networks, resource allocation with measurable financial return, and value creation and delivery at the point of execution.

Part Two

EXECUTION

How to Drive Network Management into Core Processes

We are living in a time rife with opposites. Organizations are expected to exist globally and act locally, to be efficient and innovative, and to remain profitable in both the short and long term. In this environment of increasing complexity, a one-dimensional focus is fatal. To remain competitive, leaders must satisfy investors with outstanding returns while also investing heavily in their organization's future. And their success is determined by their ability to execute, as well as by their relentless drive to improve.

Network analysis can be a vital tool in helping leaders embrace and supersede the paradoxical demands of their organization. A network perspective brings powerful new insights to execution and improvement in organizational activities such as innovation, resource allocation, and teaming. Although many organizations turn to improvement methodologies such as total quality management and Six Sigma, these methods lack a sufficiently rich provision for the social side of organizations. They discount the degree to which human relationships are critical to both short-term improvement and long-term game-changing innovation in core organizational processes. In the following chapters we reveal how ONA provides a unique advantage to leaders in recognizing the importance and necessity of effective collaborations for driving innovation and execution deep into an organization.

3

MANAGING RAPID INNOVATION THROUGH EFFECTIVE NETWORKS

The term *innovation* usually conjures up an image of a brilliant employee or sequestered team creating the next lightbulb, sticky note, or software program. Too many companies today hold to this heroic vision when, in fact, this is not how innovation usually happens. The legendary story of 3M's Post-it Notes is one of collaboration and evolution that unfolded among research scientist Spencer Silver, product developer Art Fry, and countless others. Even Thomas Edison's success depended on a team—from the fifteen engineers in his Menlo Park laboratory to financier J. P. Morgan to men such as Samuel Insull who grew the utilities that made electricity a profitable business.[15]

Consider the Apple iPod, one of the most celebrated innovations of our time. Although its elegant design has received accolades, the real innovation lies in the web of business relationships that connects hardware (Mac or PC), software (iTunes), music distributors, and even artists in ways that no other competitor has yet matched. Apple's fabled engineers saw the value of outsourcing the iPod's circuit design to a firm that had designed many of the MP3 players already on the market. These engineers also bought and built on an existing program for the iTunes software and made various decisions to reuse existing ideas in innovative ways. In so doing, Apple brought iPod to market in under eight months and demonstrated how even relatively simple innovation efforts can enjoy substantial success by fluidly tapping expertise and resources in networks inside and outside of an organization.

Apple's network strategy depends not only on hiring and promoting for individual brilliance, but also on asking leaders to mobilize networks of relevant expertise, resources, and decision-making authority. History teaches us that most breakthrough innovations are recombinations of existing ideas or technologies, the integration of which occurs through networks.[16] Now more than ever, important innovations arise from the flow of knowledge and capabilities across internal and external networks. Although traditionally these networks have formed serendipitously, it is becoming increasingly important for leaders to cultivate them in targeted ways.

United Technologies Corporation (UTC) is a heavy-equipment manufacturer composed of five dominant business units, each with a history of path-breaking innovation in its industry. A strong tenet of UTC culture has been a belief in the value of decentralized decision making, with the locus of control held by the business unit presidents and their executive teams, each challenged to achieve ambitious targets for sales and earnings growth. This structure had always worked well, but UTC chief technology officer John Cassidy and corporate research center head Carl Nett both believed that UTC was missing a tremendous opportunity for organic growth by keeping the business units isolated from each other. Integrating different kinds of expertise across business units was, in Cassidy's terms, an "unnatural act" at UTC given history, work practices, control systems, and cultural norms.

Cassidy and Nett were determined, however, and invited top technical talent from each of the divisions to two-day brainstorming sessions to decide how to bring UTC expertise together to create new products and service new markets. The intersection of cooling, heating, and power emerged early on as a potential winner. In a session outside of Paris, engineers from across UTC realized they could use the company's cooling and heating equipment to transform an innovative power-generation concept into a revolutionary product. Interestingly, the product, called PureCycle, contained virtually no major new components but rather combined existing components to provide a breakthrough value proposition, allowing customers to convert waste heat into electricity at rates substantially below those of utilities.

PureCycle takes two different heat exchangers used on large commercial air-conditioning units and couples them with a compressor converted to run as a turbine via technology adapted from UTC's Pratt & Whitney division. But instead of using electricity to produce chilled air, PureCycle takes in waste heat and produces electricity. Given that U.S. industrial plants throw away a quantity of waste heat equivalent to the production of a 160-gigawatt power plant (sufficient to power most major cities in the United States), PureCycle enjoyed a substantial market, and a payback of less than three years for many customers. Of course it is not just engineering expertise that made this product so profitable for UTC. Because PureCycle uses standard high-volume components, production costs are far below those of competitors, who must build entire systems from scratch using low-volume components. Clearly this ability to deliver a substantial innovation by repackaging existing capabilities gave UTC a significant cost advantage.

Looking back on this process today, engineers involved with PureCycle shake their heads that it took a meeting in France to identify an opportunity that was there all along. Thierry Jomard, a former Carrier engineer who transferred to the UTC research center to lead the PureCycle development effort, offers his take: "Carrier people are trained to think in terms of using heat exchange to produce cold air—that's the output that counts. The compressor is just there to move the fluid. Pratt & Whitney engineers, on the other hand, are power people—the outcome they care about is power, and they use turbines to get it." It wasn't until they came together in a brainstorming session that anyone recognized the opportunity that their combined expertise represented. Not surprisingly, moving PureCycle from idea to reality required more than the enthusiasm produced that day in France. It required bringing

UTC engineers together in a formal way and connecting their networks. "Knowing whom to call in manufacturing or finance at Carrier or in sales at Pratt has been essential," Jomard explained.

Many organizations face a similar networking challenge. They have the requisite expertise to generate substantial innovations but insufficient networks to integrate the expertise in unique ways. Internal champions such as Cassidy and Nett are often the exception rather than the rule. For every success story like PureCycle, we hear stories about ten disheartened people who did not have the formal authority or personal stamina to pull off such a coup. Too many organizations are losing time and market share by waiting for leaders like Cassidy and Nett to come along.

Network Obstacles to Innovation

Failure to innovate effectively and efficiently can often be traced to two categories of network problems: the inability to recognize opportunities and recombine expertise that is either in-house or accessible through extended networks, and the inability to test and prototype ideas rapidly when people do recognize new opportunities. The first problem is a failure to exploit expertise and networks at an organization's disposal, the second is an inability to drive change through those networks—to reshape them in ways that create value and open new markets. Both mistakes are critical because the time advantage enjoyed by successful new products has shrunk dramatically, with competitors using widespread design, manufacturing, and distribution networks to reproduce similar offerings almost overnight.

Network analysis reveals value creation possibilities that emerge simply by reconfiguring resources, expertise, and influence in existing networks. By mapping information flow, problem-solving, and decision-making networks in entire organizations or in groups charged with innovation (such as research and development, new-product development teams, or learning-oriented alliances), ONA makes visible the patterns of collaboration that either support or undermine innovation. In our work, we have found three key network obstacles to innovation in organizations:

Fragmentation. Collaboration often breaks down across functional lines, technical capabilities, and occupational subcultures in ways that invisibly undermine strategic innovation efforts.

Domination. The voices of a few central network members, who often have expertise good for times gone by, can drown out novel ideas and drive innovation efforts along traditional trajectories long after the market has veered in another direction.

Insularity. The inability to recognize and leverage relevant external expertise can yield excessive cost structures and delays that result in missed market opportunities.

These network obstacles are not new, but they are increasingly problematic in a business environment where rapid and targeted collaboration is central to innovation. A network perspective can help leaders spot and overcome these often-invisible barriers to innovation.

Fragmentation

Networks often break down precisely where leaders are counting on integration: across functions, industry or product specialties, technical competencies, and cultural values. One explanation is that people naturally gravitate to those who are like them and know similar things. But all too often network fragmentation arises from the organization's formal structure—that is, the white space in the organization chart. When this occurs, leaders need to step in to foster collaboration among those with the right expertise and influence—people who, when brought together, have a unique ability both to generate and to implement an important product or process innovation.

This scenario occurred within the R&D function of a well-known consumer products organization. This global group included thousands of scientists and high-end subject-matter experts distributed across product lines, locations, and business units. Employees reported primarily through the business units to stay in close touch with market needs. With this kind of formal structure, however, employees with similar skills and roles had few opportunities to collaborate, which in turn prevented advancements on key scientific fronts as well as best-practice transfers. To support collaboration among those with similar expertise, leadership invested heavily in an organizational infrastructure and in technology to create lateral networks, which they called communities of practice, in close to thirty expertise domains.

Over several years, evidence abounded that the strategy had proven very effective in deepening research and science in these core areas of expertise. Yet although these networks had yielded a substantial flow of incremental innovations, senior leaders saw a sharp decline in breakthrough products. They believed that new silos had formed around the communities and were preventing innovations that could come from more effective collaboration across expertise networks. They had no proof of this, however, nor could they act in a targeted fashion without better insight into the network.

To substantiate their beliefs, the group's leaders conducted an ONA, which revealed a number of troubling gaps across communities in the network. In fact, only 12 percent of the cross-community intersection points had a level of collaboration considered to be sufficient for effective innovation. Not all of these points were important to the group's innovation strategy. However, the ONA provided a clear view of close to fifty points in the global network where fragmentation was undercutting the organization's ability to generate product and process innovation breakthroughs. In some situations, members of different communities were not collaborating because they did not know where expertise was located or have a vision of how particular expertise could complement their own. In other cases, cultural barriers seemed to restrict people from seeking information outside of their own community. And in still others, basic problems with incentives, planning, and budgeting processes drove fragmentation.

Rather than applying a universal solution, such as a new technology or restructuring, which too often does *not* address the local causes of network fragmentation, leaders in this organization focused on correcting the specific drivers of collaborative breakdowns that were undermining innovation. The ability to visualize the network was critical to solving these problems and allowed leaders to address specific drivers. For example, Figure 3.1 depicts a network view of a subset of people within the polymers and packaging communities in this organization. This map reveals that four people in each community held the vast majority of relationships with key contacts in the other community. Interestingly, well over 50 percent of the ties that bridged these two communities were between low-level employees, whose integrative role in the network was a surprise to management.

Figure 3.1. Leveraging Expertise Intersections in Core Research and Development

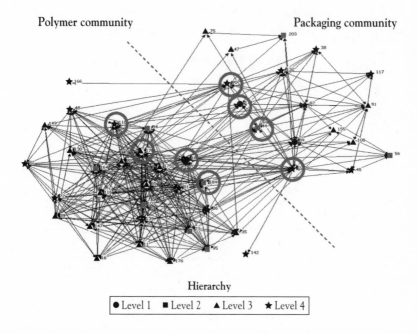

Polymer community   Packaging community

Hierarchy

● Level 1   ■ Level 2   ▲ Level 3   ★ Level 4

This insight proved extremely valuable to the top management team. As one senior leader said, "The magic of the [ONA] was identifying and helping us bring those key players together. We would have never been able to do that with our own intuition or other tools. We would have just picked people from the formal structure or people we knew, which would have been the exact wrong thing to do in hindsight as these guys are too wedded to protecting their expertise domains and not looking for integration possibilities. Also, most times they are pretty senior and are removed from the true cutting-edge ideas, where we really want to be driving innovation."

Senior managers also paid particular attention to a core set of connectors who were revealed by the ONA as having enormous impact on both overall network connectivity and ties across communities. These people's networks, leaders realized, had been undermanaged. For example, key connectors represented significant susceptibilities for the entire group; removing only 5 percent of them reduced the number of relationships in the network by more than 30 percent (see Figure 3.2). This susceptibility was extremely eye-opening because it had not been made apparent through the organization's existing talent management programs addressing looming retirements and succession planning.

Figure 3.2. Avoiding Network Fragmentation Caused by Key Departures

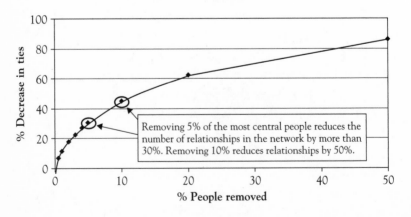

Removing 5% of the most central people reduces the number of relationships in the network by more than 30%. Removing 10% reduces relationships by 50%.

With insight into which people represented the greatest susceptibility to the network, leaders took targeted action, including paying greater attention to the key connectors and providing benefits and informal rewards that let these connectors know they were valued. Leaders also created a core high-potential program for the extreme connectors in the network, as well as a backup plan that involved staffing, career development initiatives, and rotation programs to help build connections around these people to lessen the network impact should they ever leave.

The R&D function also employed the ONA results to help community leaders glimpse the inner workings of their own groups. Many of these leaders found that their community networks, like the overall network, were fragmented, mostly across projects and tenure bands. Acting on this insight, they identified new and peripheral experts who could be drawn into key initiatives, highly central people and brokers who could forge ties across fragmentation points, and internal forums and technologies that could help build strategically important bridges.

Domination

A second network obstacle to innovation can arise when a few people dominate information and decision-making networks.[17] Effective innovation derives from more than just having the best and most relevant talent in-house. It also requires a leader to balance influence of this expertise in the network. Too often a small set of experts can dominate an entire network and drive innovation along ineffective trajectories. As one example, for much of its history Apple was run by electrical engineers and, as a result, often developed technically superior products that missed the market and were burdened by high manufacturing costs. Similarly, Microsoft's initial dismissal of the Internet stemmed in part from its history in personal computing software.

A network perspective can help managers determine if outdated paradigms are dominant and if relevant expertise is being relegated to the fringes of the network. An ONA of the R&D function of another well-known consumer products organization revealed that the expertise of people in influential network positions had a pervasive and enduring impact on the entire R&D function. In this case, the central connectors were microbiologists who had moved into highly influential network positions, creating an overly rigid informal screening process that essentially shut out ideas raised by nonmicrobiologists. As a result, many novel ideas never reached the unit's decision makers for formal consideration.

A network diagram can be used to visualize the influence of specific kinds of expertise. Figure 3.3 shows how one area of technical expertise, nutrition, was central in this R&D network and thus influenced opportunity recognition in myriad

Figure 3.3. Network Dominance of Expertise in Consumer Product Research and Development

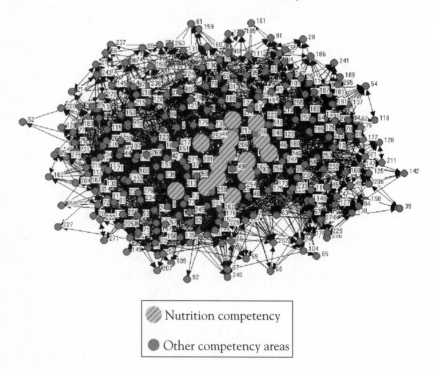

conversations that occurred outside of the formal review process. It turned out that the nutritionists, many of whom were well-regarded scientists, were overly wary of exploring new—and potentially disruptive—ideas. One such idea was low-glycemic foods (foods containing carbohydrates that digest slowly and thus make you feel full longer), which several competitors were pursuing as the next big opportunity after the low-carbohydrate craze. Rather than take what many felt was a prudent risk, the nutritionists rejected low-glycemic foods as a potential product platform. This happened not in a formal review or meeting but rather in a way that was invisible to senior leaders and decision makers. Because of these leaders' influential positions in the network, in myriad conversations and hallway interactions they screened out low-glycemic foods in a way that kept the merits and possibilities of these foods from ever rising to formal consideration.

Whereas microbiology and nutrition were overly influential in the network, other kinds of expertise, such as sensory science and quality services, were pushed to the edge. These technical competencies could yield substantial quality and efficiency benefits if they were considered early in new-product development discussions. Yet these areas had been marginalized and the experts' voices had been drowned out. Instead of being invited into problem-solving discussions, these employees were simply told what those in more central network positions required from them.

Insularity

Organizations can no longer own all the competencies and technical expertise they need for effective innovation. To reduce development time and costs, many companies outsource innovation, including research and development. For example, major pharmaceutical companies are now outsourcing 30 percent of research and 50 percent of development activities.[18] In the United States, roughly 65 to 70 percent of PDA and notebook

PC designs are being outsourced.[19] According to IBM CEO Sam Palmisano, the technological breakthrough of the Cell processor "would not have happened if we hadn't designed chips for Sony, Toshiba, Microsoft, and Nintendo . . . at the end of the day, it was through these collaborations that we were able to get this incredible breakthrough. Now we're applying that breakthrough to all sorts of places, whether it's high-definition television, consumer electronics in the home, high-definition radar systems, or medical imaging."[20]

It is increasingly important for executives to be aware of how externally sourced information and expertise migrate into the organization. A network perspective allows leaders to identify gaps and inefficiencies in how networks extend outside the organization. One such instance occurred in a pharmaceutical company that had substantial opportunities for leveraging knowledge across disease areas, such as cardiovascular conditions and asthma. Sharing effective mechanisms, results of experimental models, and late-development-stage candidates that could be used in multiple disease areas was anticipated to result in breakthrough innovation. However, leveraging research across drugs required effective collaboration both internally among research groups and externally with academic institutions, research centers, and other companies.

By applying network analysis, we discovered that although this organization had an extensive and balanced set of relationships with academic institutions, these relationships were limited to only a few people. For example, in one core therapeutic area of more than 130 scientists, just 12 of the scientists held the bulk of important external ties; in fact, removing just the top 4 of those 12 scientists reduced external connectivity by 50 percent. Because a very high percentage (80 percent) of the interactions between the pharmaceutical organization and academia were one-on-one, management needed to address how they would react if key scientists left the company (a very real concern because they were asking many high-profile scientists to relocate to a central facility as part of a major restructuring).

Another way that organizations acquire expertise is through alliances and other formal institutional relationships. Here a network perspective can reveal the trajectory of learning in external collaborations established for knowledge acquisition. For example, in the same pharmaceutical organization, we also assessed the network of an alliance intended to drive a billion dollars in sales of a drug by leveraging each organization's unique expertise in marketing, distribution, basic science, and FDA approval. Unfortunately, delays and cost overruns had all but brought the alliance to its knees. In this case, a very simple network analysis helped isolate a series of problems: ineffective distribution of decision rights, dominance of the network by one partner, lack of connections among counterparts from each organization (such as sales and manufacturing), and surprisingly strong cultural differences.

Five Practices to Drive Innovation Through Networks

Network analysis helps leaders see the barriers that undermine many organizations' ability to identify and execute innovation opportunities. We have found that successful leaders use the following five practices to overcome them:

1. *Create a network-centric ability to sense and respond to opportunities.* Innovation often derives from an ability to capitalize fluidly on new opportunities no matter where they spring up in the organization. Ideally, networks enable organizations to "surge," that is, to sense opportunities or problems in one pocket and rapidly tap into the expertise of other pockets to coordinate an effective response. This is not about pushing a greater volume of information onto employees, but about creating networks that can adapt to new problems. Building awareness of who knows what in a network is critical for people to tap the

right expertise at the right time. ONA gives leaders a map of this latent network—not the people currently being tapped for information but the people who might be when new projects or clients come along.

Various initiatives can help increase awareness of who knows what. On a technical front, skill-profiling systems, social network technologies, and even well-structured "wikis" can generate awareness of expertise throughout a group without overloading employees with information. To be most effective, technologies such as a skill-profiling system are built into the organization's workflows so that people can keep their expertise profiles up-to-date and relevant. These systems also become more valuable when organizations include information that inspires trust. When an employee consults a colleague who is a complete stranger, some level of trust in the person's expertise and ability is critical. The elements that rapidly generate trust differ across organizations; for example, in some places academic degrees are important while in others experience is all that counts. What matters is including the information that creates legitimacy in a particular organization.

Other companies and government organizations have focused more on face-to-face interactions to help build awareness of expertise. Many organizations we have worked with have used awareness network diagrams (network diagrams based not on who is getting information from whom at a given point in time but rather on who understands the skills and expertise of colleagues throughout an organization) to redesign staffing or rotation programs, which is a fairly cost-effective way to create awareness across critical network divides. Pharmaceutical organizations, for example, employ innovative rotation programs to help create awareness of expertise between their marketing and R&D organizations. Another common solution is some kind of off-site or annual meeting. In these efforts, understanding the awareness network helps leaders revise meeting formats to enhance the network's ability to surge.

Consider the R&D function discussed earlier in which innovation was stalling because certain expertise had become overly prominent in the network. As part of a broader effort to improve collaboration throughout the R&D function, management held an off-site meeting to help build connectivity across R&D projects. Of course, many of us have gone to off-site or all-hands meetings only to engage with people we already know. Quite often such events serve to entrench networks rather than expand them at points that matter for the organization. But in this case, efforts were taken at every step to ensure that bridges were built across gaps that the network analysis revealed were impeding innovation. Everything from how tables were staffed and then rotated to the kinds of problem-solving sessions people participated in was geared toward building connectivity with a potential payoff rather than just mingling in order to build an ad hoc network.

One of the most interesting activities involved the use of an electronic name tag that people were given as they headed off for drinks and dinner at the end of the first day. These electronic badges had the ability to communicate with every other badge in the room, so they helped broker introductions—but not just any introductions. We programmed two things into each tag: the person's existing network and the skills to which that person needed access in order to help the organization innovate along strategically important trajectories. As a person moved around the room, if her tag sensed that she was near another person who was both outside her network and had the requisite expertise, it would light up and flash a welcome to the other person: *Hi Bob. We should be talking about biochemistry.* In this way, the tags brokered introductions that were task based and value added for the organization, instead of perpetuating the "more is better" approach to connectivity.

What was fun in this case was that if two people stayed connected to each other for a while beyond the initial introduction, a network link between them would be logged with the name tags. This link was then transported to the front of the room, appearing on two very large screens on which people could see the network taking shape in two-minute increments. In addition to adding a sense of energy to the room, this visual element gave the head of R&D a baseline of potential value-added connections to explore. In six and then nine months, he was able to assess which connections had endured beyond the event and whether they were bearing any fruit, as well as invest in the relationships and ideas that were important but for one reason or another had not paid off.

Although the name tag technology is fun, it can often represent more effort than many organizations want to invest in an off-site meeting—and it is certainly too much for regular operational meetings. In these and other cases, there is still a tremendous amount a leader can do to understand and shape the awareness network. A simple but highly effective practice is to invite peripheral experts to a meeting to talk about a challenge or key win they have recently experienced. Alternatively, fun brainstorming sessions can emerge—in either face-to-face meetings or collaborative spaces—when leaders simply pose the question, *What would happen if we integrated expertise at certain points in the network?* These sessions are most effective when targeted at points in the network that are breaking down but where leaders see potential in integrating expertise.

2. *Develop an ability to rapidly test and refine an opportunity.* Effective innovation is about action as much as vision. Companies that execute well on innovation have a network that can rapidly combine and deploy resources to test many opportunities. Sony's inability to create a successful product for the portable MP3 player market—a market they dominated for decades with the Walkman—was a failure not of vision but of action. By the time Apple introduced the iPod, the market for digital music players was already taking its first steps. Napster was infamous for enabling online music sharing, jukebox software was already organizing the digital music files on PCs, and

portable MP3 players were already on the market. Sony engineers and executives saw these opportunities at the same time as the team at Apple did, but Apple was able to mobilize networks of expertise, resources, and decision-making authority to jump on the opportunity while Sony was not, despite having entire divisions devoted to the Walkman, the personal computer, and even music labels.

Organizations need to be able to explore emerging opportunities rapidly. The shift from envisioning a single future to testing a range of possible futures relies on the ability of leaders to mobilize networks of expertise fluidly and then build and test innovations using resources inside and sometimes outside of the organization. In some cases, this means having programmers or a model shop ready to turn an idea into a functioning prototype. In one company, we created an informal model shop where employees, from engineers to marketing executives, could rapidly mock up their ideas. This physical space has now become a venue for networks to form to enable novel insights to be generated and tested.

The ability to prototype can also be supported by trusted suppliers, who can quickly provide new and promising materials or design changes, or by retail partners, who can make shelf space available for a brief test of the market. One company we worked with used their supplier's retail stores to test-market new products quickly and easily—getting feedback not only from customers but also from store managers and staff. The ability to rapidly prototype and test a new offering is critical to gaining proof of concept, learning, and success stories that enable innovations to gain momentum in a network.

Mapping decision-making networks also yields important means for helping an organization to innovate. When decision rights—who can make what kind of decision—are unclear, every issue must be pushed up the hierarchy, creating bottlenecks and sapping the energy of those with innovative insights. Decision-making networks can quickly reveal where certain decision rights need to be defined or reallocated to allow for more rapid prototyping of ideas. Once changes have been made in decision rights, an ONA can also reveal whether employees are starting to act on their own initiative or continue to seek approval for everything they do. Several executives we have worked with have used decision-making networks to identify people in central network positions and encourage them to take prudent risks—an approach that helps fight fear and promote creativity in a targeted and personal way that diffuses through the network.

3. *Work through people in specific network positions.* People in privileged positions in their organization's information networks—who are not always or even usually high in the formal hierarchy—can have a substantial impact on how an innovative idea is developed and implemented. Typically, senior managers looking to initiate brainstorming or problem-solving sessions simply invite the people they know or like. Consider Figure 3.4, a mocked-up diagram used here to represent people whom leaders are likely to select for an innovation effort if formal position is their guide. Unfortunately, these people are not the best choices. They are central only in their own groups, are most likely to be wedded to a certain way of doing things, may not have a good sense of the capabilities of individuals outside their immediate network, and are not necessarily influential in other groups with which they might need to coordinate efforts.

Now consider the people in Figure 3.5. Their network positions make them aware of resources and expertise dispersed throughout an organization, and they are more likely than others to be successful at crafting a viable solution because of their understanding of the political dynamics and cultural values in various subgroups. Interestingly, these brokers are often not well known by the leaders of an organization because they sit in the white space between pockets of a network. Typically, leaders are able to guess only about 30 percent of the key brokers in a network and thus are often not leveraging a critical resource in their organization.

Figure 3.4. Group Managers as Innovation Influencers

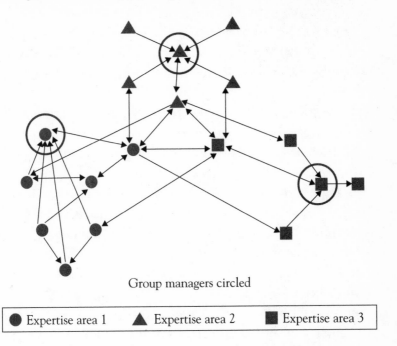

Group managers circled

| ● Expertise area 1 | ▲ Expertise area 2 | ■ Expertise area 3 |

Figure 3.5. Key Brokers as Innovation Influencers

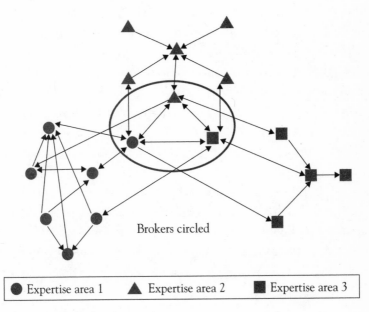

Brokers circled

| ● Expertise area 1 | ▲ Expertise area 2 | ■ Expertise area 3 |

An ONA can help leaders identify brokers like those in Figure 3.5, who hold the entire network together by virtue of their relationships across subgroups and formal structure. An ONA can also help identify those with expertise relevant to a given innovation. Coloring nodes (people) in the network according to technical competency and finding those most sought out for expertise that is relevant to an innovation identifies employees with both technical depth and credibility in the eyes of their peers—attributes that are important to both the development and the implementation of a new idea.

As important as bringing the right people into the room is engaging a diversity of people. Involving a variety of experts in the inception of an idea is critical both to its quality and to the ease of implementation. In the words of one senior technology executive, "A sure way that innovation has consistently failed here for decades is for ideas to be developed in isolation. No matter how right or good they might be, it is the most consistent death knell to an initiative." Brokers are needed in this case to reach out to other key connectors in the network to assess and improve a solution before people have become wedded to it, and then to address implementation obstacles that people brainstorming in a room by themselves might not have identified.

4. *Leverage energy.* Up to this point we have focused on networks solely in terms of information flow and decision making. Yet it turns out that emotion plays a substantial role in determining who people learn from—particularly when someone is looking for answers to new problems. Mapping enthusiasm in networks simply by asking people to indicate who makes them feel energized (and who is a drain) provides a powerful indicator of where creativity and innovation are occurring. As one executive said, "You have to be energizing to get people to listen to your idea to begin with, and certainly energizing to get them to help you implement it or accept it. Nothing gets done here, it seems, without someone somewhere getting enthused about an idea and then enthusing others."

A simple addition to an ONA, network diagrams of enthusiasm can highlight where energy is high and where creativity and effective collaboration are likely to occur. Focusing on these points can be a quick way to gain ground on both planned and emerging innovation opportunities. Similarly, these diagrams help reveal people who are energizing others in the network; leaders often see great returns from providing these emergent leaders with room and resources as ways to leverage the natural flow of ideas in a network. And of course de-energizing networks can help a leader locate and work with those who have an uncanny ability to suck the life out of a group.

Once leaders find such opportunities for improvement, they can then help foster energizing behaviors. These behaviors, which our interviews have revealed to be consistently associated with generating positive energy,[21] can be developed through coaching, career development processes, embedding behavioral dimensions in project or team evaluations, or simple self-assessments. Wherever energy is lagging, contemplating the following five questions can result in subtle changes that have a dramatic impact. Although it's difficult to convert extreme de-energizers (those whose negativity is tied up with their basic personality), it's entirely possible to help those who just need to change some fairly simple behaviors.

- *Do you do what you say you are going to do and address tough issues with integrity?* People are energized in the presence of others who stand for something larger than themselves. Reservations fall away and enthusiasm builds when people can trust that others will follow through on commitments.

- *Do you see realistic possibilities in conversations and avoid focusing too early or heavily on potential obstacles?* People get enthused in the presence of attainable possibilities. De-energizers claim they are playing the devil's advocate, but by raising only problems and never venturing solutions, they keep ideas from getting off the ground.

- *Are you mentally and physically engaged in meetings and conversations?* Energizers are not necessarily wildly charismatic, but they are always fully present in conversations. Rather than going through the motions of being engaged—something that is much more transparent than de-energizers think—they show their interest in the person and the topic by bringing themselves fully into a given interaction.

- *Are you flexible in your thinking and do you use your expertise appropriately?* Too often, in their haste to find a solution or demonstrate their knowledge, experts or leaders destroy energy. People want to be a part of something meaningful. Energizers create a sense of purpose in others by drawing them into conversations and projects.

- *When you disagree, do you focus on the issue at hand rather than on the individual?* Energizers are quick to disagree when things go off track, but they do so in a way that does not tie their critique of a suggestion too tightly to the person who made it. Their approach allows a continued improvement in the idea and also avoids marginalizing the person and his or her contribution to the conversation.

5. *Ensure that organizational context supports collaboration.* Effective collaboration is a holistic challenge. Simply introducing a collaborative technology, tweaking incentives, or advocating cultural programs to boost collaboration is insufficient. Promoting connectivity requires the alignment of unique aspects of formal organizational design, control systems, technology, and human resource practices. In addition to organizational design, specific cultural values and leadership behavior can have striking effects on patterns of collaboration.

What needs to change depends on the organization. In some settings, battling an entrenched cultural value can be critical; in others, modifying division-level planning processes and performance metrics is central to improving a network. For example, recently a top IBM executive publicly criticized the firm's reward structures, which pitted divisions against one another: "We don't talk to people in other operations. They have become the competition. There is no sharing of information and [there is] limited cooperation."[22] In our own work, we have seen collaboration between R&D groups stall because it took longer to get approval to transfer human resources from one project to another than to get the work done.

Although executives will not be able to overhaul organizations entirely to create the ideal collaborative context, they can at least make sure that fragmentation across certain aspects of formal structure or physical location is not impeding innovation. One company created formal "dual-citizenship" roles to allow someone in research and development to collaborate with others in the business units without requiring internal budget transfers or formal project reassignments. It may also be useful to create ad hoc teams around particular organizational capabilities in order to spread the cost structure across more than one business unit. Within Hewlett-Packard, for example, a small team developed an expertise in supply chain management. By working with different divisions and plants to optimize local supply chains, this group moved best ideas and practices across divisions that had been rivals. 3M has also developed technology labs in this way; rather than hope that the divisions would learn from each other, they made it the charter of these labs to move ideas across organizational boundaries.

The entire human resources chain can affect collaboration by informing the kinds of people who are brought into the organization, the way they are developed, and the behaviors that are measured and rewarded. IDEO, one of the largest and most successful design and innovation firms, has developed an employee evaluation process that is driven by feedback from those the employee has worked *with*, not just *for*, on the employee's own projects and on other projects. Project teams at IDEO are usually able to choose their members, creating an informal reward system that identifies who is collaborative and who is out for themselves.

Conclusion

The major barriers to innovation result not from failures of individual genius but from failures of collaboration—the inability to exploit existing capabilities in revolutionary ways. Having the right talent in place—a substantial challenge in and of itself—is just the first step. Effective leaders need to be aware of how skills and abilities are distributed, and tapped, within the networks that make up their organization. In an increasingly dynamic business environment, those who can read and harness the networks in and beyond their organizations, quickly diagnose breakdowns in those networks before they become crises, and effectively build new networks around emerging innovations will enjoy the greatest success.

In this chapter we have shown ways that a network perspective can help leaders efficiently spur innovation. A series of actions can unleash innovation potential:

1. Leaders need to shift efforts to spur innovation along specific trajectories from individual or team-based initiatives to activities that reshape networks. Rather than just sequestering teams and demanding innovation, leaders can recognize substantial innovations by uniquely integrating expertise and resources that are accessible through networks within and outside of their organizations.

2. Once desired trajectories of innovation are defined, leaders can apply network analysis to assess and correct three common network barriers to innovation:

    Fragmentation: Collaborative breakdowns across functional lines, technical capabilities, and occupational subcultures

Domination: Central network members invisibly screening out novel ideas

Insularity: Lack of external ties needed to recognize and leverage expertise outside the organization

3. Network analysis can also promote the quality and feasibility of new product, process, or service ideas generated. This chapter has shown how targeted investments in building awareness of expertise and energy in networks yields greater creative capacity. In addition, staffing employees who are well situated in information and expertise networks on key projects can dramatically improve the quality and feasibility of an innovation.

4. In terms of implementation, failure to innovate effectively and efficiently can often be traced to the inability to test and prototype ideas rapidly. Rather than being a failure to exploit the expertise and networks that are at the organization's disposal, this is an inability to drive change through those networks—to reshape them in ways that create value and open new markets. Making decision-making networks visible and leveraging key network players at appropriate points in new-product development processes—as described in this chapter—can dramatically improve innovation success.

4

DRIVING FINANCIAL RETURN THROUGH NETWORK INVESTMENTS

The challenge in deriving value from networks is to know how much to invest and where to allocate resources. Research on social networks has tended to focus on relationships as instrumental ties—task-related communication, information flow, work flow, or decision making[23]—but has ignored the value that is created through these interactions. With a slight shift in perspective, leaders can better understand how interactions in networks generate economic return—a very different sense of where value is created or cost incurred than is conveyed in traditional financial reports and budgeting processes.

Halliburton—one of the world's largest providers of products and services to the petroleum and energy industries—has regularly employed ONA in many of its efforts to build nineteen networks across a variety of business units and technical services. These networks—which Halliburton calls Communities of Practice—were each strategically designed to show measurable results directly linked to financial performance. For example, employees in one global network of engineers (the completions community) design, manufacture, and install equipment that enables the production of hydrocarbons from newly completed oil and gas wells. Final design of a completed well depends heavily on the well's operational parameters. This means that a completion may go through many changes depending on how the drilling of the well develops, on the various reservoirs it may cross, on expected production, and on local logistics. Because of this dynamic environment, all those involved must collaborate closely to avoid errors in handoffs from one group to the next.

Halliburton created a global community to help engineers find cost and time-saving solutions for designing individual wells that could be replicated at drilling sites around the world. The effectiveness of this newly formed network was tested early on when an engineer experienced a problem with a deep-water well in West Africa. Through both virtual forums and specialist roles in the network, the community found a solution to the problem, which then saved time and money on three other completions to be performed within the next twenty-four hours. As a result of this kind of collaborative problem solving and best-practice transfer, the community ended up saving millions of dollars for important customers during its pilot phase.

A network analysis of these engineers proved integral to establishing the community of practice because it allowed management to take targeted actions to improve community effectiveness. For example, the ONA helped senior managers identify some very knowledgeable and experienced people who were not well engaged in solving problems outside their area of operations. It also revealed three technical advisers who were so consumed by repetitive and mundane requests from the field that they had no time left for capturing and sharing best practices. And it helped to uncover network silos that were driving sharp increases in the cost of poor quality.

For example, U.S. operations in the Gulf of Mexico had developed several new practices and, as a result, decreased the cost of poor quality in Gulf operations by 50 percent in twelve months. Yet during that same time frame, the rest of the countries involved in the ONA had experienced a 13 percent *increase* in the cost of poor quality. As a result, senior executives made sure that experienced people were tapped as "knowledge champions" across the community. These people became the first point of contact for all others with questions in a given domain—a role that allowed them to be much more aware than others of how to connect knowledge seekers and experts in the network, as well as allowing them to ensure diffusion of best practices throughout the group as soon as they were uncovered.

Management at Halliburton supported collaboration by also implementing a series of organizational and technical changes to improve knowledge transfer. For example, organizationally, the network analysis informed several rotations of high-potential employees between select countries to offer professional development opportunities for the individuals and to establish connections between previously unconnected regions. Technologically, a skill-profiling system was also installed to decrease the time it took for community members to get answers and solutions (dramatically shrinking time from thirty days to an average of three days).

Importantly, the ONA allowed Halliburton to focus collaboration investments in a way that generated value for the organization. These and other highly targeted efforts led to substantial business results that more than justified the investments. By transferring best practices among regions, the community increased revenues by 22 percent in one year while lowering the cost of poor quality by 66 percent. In addition, productivity measures improved by 10 percent while customer dissatisfaction ratings dropped by 24 percent. A follow-up network analysis performed one year later revealed overall improvement in the network as well. For example, cohesion—a network measure of the average number of steps it takes for each person in the community to get to every other person—improved by nearly 25 percent. This improvement, combined with field observations, made clear to Halliburton that important business conversations were occurring without imposing an unnecessary collaborative burden on all.

Driving Value Creation Relationally

Halliburton's success in creating communities of practice shows that well-considered network investments generate measurable return by increasing *productive* interactions and reducing *unproductive* ones. Another opportunity to influence value creation comes from applying network analysis to assess value creation and cost relationally in the myriad collaborations that occur within a network. Throughout our work we have seen a network lens help drive economic value creation into network interactions by:

- Revealing collaborations that are central to productivity improvement and modeling anticipated returns from network investments

- Assessing collaborations that underlie revenue generation and replicating these interactions at value-added points in a network

- Visualizing cost structures relationally to improve efficiency through a more accurate understanding of the magnitude and drivers of collaborative costs

Network Contributions to Productivity Improvement

One way of assessing value creation relationally is to determine how much time people save when they receive resources and expertise through a network to which they would not otherwise have access. Figure 4.1 depicts a bar chart of time savings arising from information and other resources shared among project managers in a global financial services organization. Those at the bottom of the chart made substantial contributions that boosted their colleagues' productivity; those near the top made marginal contributions or none at all. Quite often, leaders find that a previously unrecognized employee is more central to the network than they had thought, and vice versa. In these cases, people revealed as central contributors—those who are highly

Figure 4.1. Translating Time-Saving Interactions into Economic Return

Savings/Quarter

regarded by their peers and are not just currying favor with the boss—are often flagged for inclusion in high-potential leadership programs, become more prominent in succession planning, and are tasked to assume substantive roles in a redesign.

Aggregating results by business units, roles, projects, or hierarchical levels can reveal broader insights about where organization-wide investments in networks need to be increased or reduced. In this example, the network of project managers distributed around the world generated savings of 3,383 hours in a single month (converting to roughly $215,000 at the average loaded compensation). Most of this value was created in collaborations within business units; only $67,500 came from interactions across units. Unfortunately, this figure was substantially below leaders' expectations; the business case for forming and supporting this expert network had been based on realizing time savings and best-practice transfers from collaborations across functional lines and physical distance. Because this network of project managers was one of more than twenty networks that revealed this kind of shortfall, it became clear that investments needed to be redirected in order to focus employees on cross-unit collaborations that would generate synergies and minimize replication of effort.

But how much time, technology, or other resources should be applied to promote connectivity? In this case, network analysis allowed leaders to weigh the anticipated costs and benefits of such investments. Connecting the key brokers and getting each of them to engage one peripheral person proved to be an easy and effective way to promote desired cross-business unit connectivity. Such simple steps were anticipated to yield $140,000 a year in savings through enhanced collaborations within business units, and $865,000 through cross-unit collaborations— returns that even if overestimated by an order of magnitude still more than outweighed the anticipated investment of a new collaborative technology and a portion of employees' time.

Network views can help leaders make informed financial investments to promote value-added collaboration. They are also helpful in tracking the return generated from network investments over time. For example, another leading multinational petrochemical company continually uses network analysis to assess the value of collaboration in its exploration and production business. In an industry with highly compensated experts and large investments in fixed assets, avoiding problems—or at least reducing the time it takes to solve them— is critical. To promote sharing of best practices across disciplines such as production, drilling, geology, and geophysics, the company formed more than twenty-five expert networks, ranging from fifty to several hundred employees, based on work areas that could benefit from the healthy exchange of best practices.

One network formed around the monitoring of turbo machines, enormous pieces of equipment that provide pressure and suction for oil extraction. Three core team members were identified to lead the network, and they in turn nominated other well-connected people who could represent various business units.

The organization then used ONA to assess and improve the health of these groups and to determine how much was being saved through the transfer of best practices. The network analysis also collected stories about important cost savings, both to validate the time-savings estimate and to share within the broader organization to encourage further cost savings. Because of the returns generated within and outside of the community, these network leaders were never questioned on budget requests for meetings, technology support, or other collaborative efforts, such as after-action reviews—initiatives that, prior to the use of ONA, had always been immediately cut from budget requests and labeled frivolous.

Revealing Collaborations That Generate Revenue

Leaders can help drive organic growth by assessing and improving collaborations that are central to revenue creation. In most organizations it is rare for sales of importance to be delivered through the individual effort of a single account leader, client partner, managing director, or sales executive operating on his or her own. Although stories of individual heroic accomplishments circulate too often, it is almost always the case that successful sales occur as a product of networks that help materialize a range of expertise and resources. Unfortunately, most leaders do not have accurate pictures of these collaborations and too often undermine important networks by measuring and rewarding individual results. In these cases, network analysis can help drive revenue by (1) identifying collaborative breakdowns across offerings where integration can yield competitive differentiation or more holistic solutions, (2) revealing where uncoordinated efforts with key clients undermine overall account potential, and (3) uncovering stars who contribute much more to an organization's top line than individually focused sales metrics might suggest.

One investment bank used network analysis to help bring to market a greater breadth of the firm's expertise. To execute global growth plans and compete with the premiere banks in its peer group, this institution needed networks that could mobilize expertise seamlessly across industry and product lines in response to client opportunities. To build these critical connections, the bank used ONA to assess revenue-producing collaborations *among* the client-facing managing director population and then *between* this group and other key employees in the organization. Conducting the ONA in this way enabled leaders to see how the members of the global network of managing directors were leveraging one another's abilities, as well as whether this key group was being effectively supported by the broader organization via several thousand managing directors and senior vice presidents in critical support and decision roles.

Unfortunately, despite the need for lateral connectivity to support a "one-firm" strategy, our results showed that revenue-producing collaborations were heavily focused first within divisions and then within regions. Three initiatives helped to bridge these strategically important network gaps. First, targeted efforts at select intersections in the network (for example, fixed income and equities) helped promote connectivity through revised account-planning practices, rotation programs, and brainstorming sessions that brought together well-connected people from each region. Second, each divisional leader focused on his or her unit's network and on ways in which the connectivity of their high performers could be broadened, as well as on how the leader could coordinate more effectively with other divisions on a top-fifty account list. Third, specific attention was focused on leveraging brokers in the network—those people who did not necessarily have the most connections overall but who did have the most ties across divisions and regions. Steps were taken to better utilize the top 5 percent of these brokers, who held more than 30 percent of the critical cross-division collaborations, via coordinated sales efforts and by systematically building these brokering roles into aspects of formal structure.

In addition to correcting network fragmentation, we also found that revenue-generating ties were focused on a small number of people; only 10 percent of the managing directors supported almost 50 percent of the revenue-producing collaborations. This excessive reliance on a small number of managing directors created a tremendous susceptibility should these key players leave the organization, because these people were highly influential in supporting other employees and held key connections with the firm's largest accounts. Interestingly, although some of the key revenue enablers were well known by senior leaders, others were substantial surprises.

In fact, the firm's top talent list overlapped with the key revenue generators in the network by only about 30 percent. This finding was eye-opening in helping the organization hone in on key talent they had not been aware of, as well as in beginning to rethink what key talent was in the first place. Rather than focusing on just individual production, the network lens let leaders begin to see and place value on those players who made their colleagues more effective. Strategically, this change enabled the firm to cultivate networks that yielded more than the sum of the individual contributors, and created a multiplier effect by getting greater leverage out of top talent.

Of course, not all central people play productive roles in a network. In organizations, people tend to become central in networks in two ways. Some become highly connected by virtue of their formal role—by the decisions they get to make, the resources they get to dole out, and the information to which they are privy. Others become central by virtue of who they are as people—they are sought out for their expertise, client contacts, and general personal leadership skills. In this case, we used the network analysis to further clarify the key benefits that people obtained from others in revenue-focused collaborations. This process let us see those employees who were central because of their position in the organization, and those who were central because of their individual qualities of expertise or their industry contacts.

Two critical points came from this insight. First, as seen in Figure 4.2, it turned out that most of the people whom the managing directors claimed to need more access to in order to be more effective turned out to be other managing directors who were central largely due to the decisions they made. In other words, in this network, bottlenecks were emerging where a small set of people were not making decisions in a timely fashion. Simple shifts in role definition, decision processes, and frequency of and attendance at key decision meetings were implemented to improve the overall ability of this network to execute.

Second, for those directors who were central as a product of their expertise and client relationships, the network analysis helped reveal behaviors and individual connections that enabled these employees to become highly central and productive. Once the skills and network profiles of these high performers were understood, they became competencies around which the organization could design talent and performance management

Figure 4.2. Role- and Non-Role-Driven Driven Collaborations

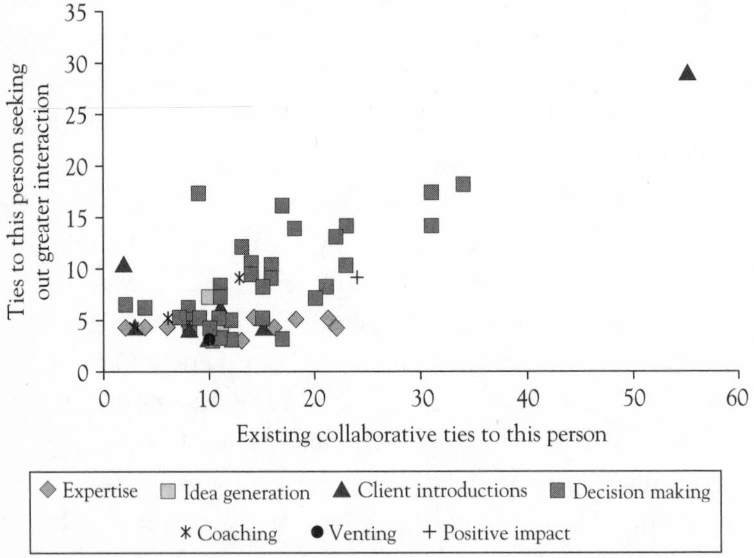

Note: The data points are the top 5 percent of the most-sought-out people in the network, coded by most prominent benefit.

processes. In terms of performance management, these behaviors became a component of post-project evaluations. In terms of skill development, the network profiles and behaviors were implemented into a range of talent processes from onboarding to 360-degree evaluations to leadership development efforts.

In addition to the well-connected employees, it was equally interesting to note that close to 20 percent of the managing directors who were identified as top performers turned out to provide little or no collaborative support to their peers. Although they were individually productive, many of these employees lived on the fringe of the network and did not enable the bank to leverage their abilities. As a result, many of these employees became focal points for coaching, while other peripheral managing directors received greater attention in onboarding. As you would expect, it turned out that tenure had a lot to do with many who were on the periphery. People who had been around longer had had more time to develop trusted ties. Yet a select group of managing directors had become well-connected very quickly, so interviews were used to help clarify the behaviors of these fast movers and to make specific changes to onboard experienced hires more effectively.

In short, being able to assess revenue production in networks enabled this organization to make unique and targeted improvements to key talent programs that in turn boosted revenue and account penetration. Every investment bank pursues cross-selling, but they all also contend with bonus schemes that dramatically deincentivize people to collaborate with those in other product and industry groups. In this case, the network analysis enabled leaders to replicate the behaviors and networks of those who contributed most to sales efforts without trying to battle entrenched performance management systems. It also enabled the organization to revise talent processes in order to address four key questions: (1) What do the most effective managing directors do through their networks that invisibly enable sales, and how can we replicate these networks and behaviors more rapidly throughout the workforce? (2) What susceptibilities do highly central managing directors create, and how can we use talent and account planning processes to mitigate revenue impact on these peoples' departures? (3) Who are the high performers who are not supporting their colleagues, and what can be done to help ensure that the organization gets appropriate leverage from their contacts and expertise? and (4) How can we best create targeted cross-function and distance collaborations that will yield superior capabilities in assembling expertise for sales purposes?

Visualizing the Costs of Collaboration

Finally, network analysis can also be very effective in understanding collaborative costs throughout an organization. Reflect for a moment on your typical work week. In that mythical week, what percentage of your time do you spend in meetings, on telephone calls, and responding to e-mails? A survey we conducted through The Network Roundtable indicated most estimates to be between 65 and 85 percent, with those higher in the hierarchy sometimes exceeding 95 percent, to the point of planning their calendars in fifteen-minute increments. Clearly a substantial portion of time at work is consumed in a wide range of collaborations. Given the magnitude of this time, it is curious that leaders rarely, if ever, assess the efficiency of these network interactions.

Most of us can relate to scenarios where we have seen phenomenal amounts of time consumed in network interactions to gain agreement on a simple course of action, navigate a bureaucracy on an obvious decision, or endure unhelpful colleagues who—not satisfied with being unproductive on their own—have to waste the time of many others in endless meetings and conversations. We tend to accept these interactions as inevitable and simply to be lived through. But consider what might be done if we could assess and then improve the efficiency of these interactions. Clearly we can't hope to remove all or even most of the time spent in these collaborations, but imagine what we or our organization might do if we could secure a 10 percent or even a 20 percent improvement in the efficiency of these networks.

Assessing how time is spent in collaborations and then multiplying this time by loaded compensation figures helps leaders to understand the magnitude and drivers of collaborative costs in networks. Viewing costs this way always reveals specific individuals who absorb the time and energy of many others—thereby imposing a substantial drain on the network that more often than not far outweighs the value that the individual generates. Colleagues who do not execute commitments, leaders who routinely revisit and reverse decisions, bureaucrats who enjoy picking apart plans, and experts who simply won't make themselves sufficiently available to others are just a few of the people who come to mind. In these instances, network analysis can offer a powerful means to illuminate and correct behaviors that impose substantial inefficiencies on organizations but traditionally have remained invisible.

Beyond individuals, leaders can also begin to place a cost on the cultural aspects of a network. For example, we have used these views to demonstrate how lack of trust in a recently merged group drove excessive cost structures through multiple decision processes and meetings where key employees were not forthcoming with critical concerns. Alternatively, in another organization we used network analysis to reveal the "cost of fear" that leaders in the organization had created. By this we of course don't mean that employees were physically scared of their leaders, but rather that they feared public reprimand, private reprisal, and career consequences of taking risks to such a degree that they drove three costly network dynamics.

First, employees would not venture into substantial interactions outside of their units without elevating requests up through their leaders for fear that their leaders would be surprised. Of course, because this drove leaders to be overloaded, cross-unit collaborations rarely, if ever, occurred. Unfortunately, this dynamic flew in the face of the CEO's strategy to deliver a market premium to shareholders through organic growth and a one-firm culture that could yield synergies and cross-selling of products across business units only if networks were laterally connected. In this case, we used network analysis to see where and how collaborative time was spent, and we specifically focused on those collaborations that consumed four hours or more a month (assuming that a minimum of one hour a week would be important to establish cross-organizational efforts). An eye-opening result for the leaders occurred when they found that 86 percent of the collaborations among the top 210 leaders were still mired within business units. Viewed this way, it became clear that alterations to formal structure and incentives had not sufficiently outweighed the political costs that employees feared.

Second, and even more troubling for this organization, was the extent to which collaborative time was directed up the hierarchy because employees would not take action on ideas without double- and sometimes triple-checking with their leaders. This was a pervasive problem in the network, but for our purposes here we focus on one clear opportunity with the executive team. When we looked at time consumed by various roles in the network, it turned out that the members of the top management team were substantial drains on the overall network. On average, each of these leaders consumed 190 hours a month of other leaders' time in one-on-one and group meetings. This was a significant drain to the organization resource-wise and made visible the importance of the top team letting go of routine decisions such as simple promotion and pay raises, travel approvals, and pricing.

Third, interviews brought into focus the cultural and leadership-behavior components of these costs as well. One more junior member of the top 210 leaders put it in clear perspective: "The network results definitely showed that we are hierarchical in decision making and that we can put a real cost to that in ways that have finally captured the attention of our leaders. Before, I think they thought we were grousing and they of course did not want to give up control of things—and neither would I, probably, if I were in their shoes. But this has forced the conversation to the forefront and helped shift certain decisions down to where they should be. What is even more interesting is that it has motivated the cultural question of intimidation, and by that I mean people overpreparing for meetings or keeping all but bulletproof ideas silent. We easily spend four to five times the amount of time you have shown in preparation for meetings. So the cost of our hierarchical tendency is really enormous when you factor in both this prep time and the opportunity cost of so many good ideas not getting voiced."

Beyond cultural tendencies, however, substantial collaborative inefficiencies often result from outdated role definitions or ineffective decision-right allocation. For example, consider a network analysis we conducted in the information technology organization of a leading utility. The CIO wanted a better understanding of how collaboration among certain roles affected the IT department's decisions and the efficiency of its work, so we assessed interaction time in the network and then converted time to cost using a loaded hourly rate. The results are presented in Table 4.1, which is read from row to column and shows *average monthly* costs of collaboration *per employee* within a given role as well as between roles throughout the group. The rows denote the average labor cost for all employees in each role. For example, for the seventeen application architects, the average loaded labor cost per employee for interaction time with those in the same role was $2,126—denoted "internal"—and the average labor costs for time spent with those in other roles ranged from $476 to $1,597, with a total cost per employee for interaction time with "external" roles of $5,638.

Although it might seem overly detailed, this view of work offers leaders two important insights on collaborative time and

Table 4.1. Labor Cost of Time Spent in Interactions with Others

Role title	Number of Employees	Average Cost for Interaction Time, per Employee, per Month										Total
		Application Architect	Business Unit Architect	Data Architect	Infrastructure Architect	Systems Analyst	Project Manager	Other	Overall	Internal	External	Monthly interaction labor costs
Application Architect	17	$2,126	$1,121	$715	$1,597	$476	$626	$1,103	$7,765	$2,126	$5,638	$132,000
Business Unit Architect	5	3,750	2,460	1,110	1,560	30	210	660	9,780	2,460	7,320	48,900
Data Architect	6	3,600	950	2,800	2,225	225	975	650	11,425	2,800	8,625	68,550
Infrastructure Architect	16	1,406	656	375	5,588	56	1,013	1,069	10,163	5,588	4,575	162,600
Systems Analyst	2	1,125	0	150	975	0	1,500	1,275	5,025	0	5,025	10,050
Project Manager	5	1,680	210	1,050	3,180	1,680	1,470	3,450	12,720	1,470	11,250	63,600
Other	7	1,714	471	193	1,843	364	1,971	2,057	8,614	2,057	6,557	60,300

cost structures. First, in terms of formal structure, it provides substantial insight into the collaborative demands of given roles and thus helps organizations more effectively fund, design, recruit, and train for these roles. Too often, technical people—such as the ones the CIO was concerned about—are simply assessed and developed for their technical knowledge and not for their critical ability to interact effectively across formal lines. Second, these views enable much more accurate allocation of costs to key projects or functions in organizations. Traditionally, costs are assigned to a given project or department on the basis of where a person is housed or allocating time. But in reality some roles—such as the project managers in this organization—consume the time of a great many other people in the network. As a result, traditional budgeting practices can substantially underestimate the cost of functions in organizations or of roles on a given project. When considering just one project, this is not a big deal. But when assessing resource allocation in an entire department or business unit composed of dozens of projects, the effect can be substantial and alter which project would be undertaken, depending on the organization's desired rates of return.

For the CIO, this analysis revealed two views of resource allocation that no traditional budgeting or cost-allocation processes could provide. First, it turned out that the cost of collaboration, measured as employees' time, was much higher for some roles than for others. Sometimes these costs were justified. Infrastructure architects, for instance, define the technical direction and standards for the entire department. Given the importance of standardization and consistency among architectures, over half of their collaborative costs came from interactions with other infrastructure architects. But in other cases, there were clear opportunities to reduce collaboration costs and redefine roles. For example, the network results showed that data architects and project managers spent almost half of their time in interactions with IT coworkers, yet these very real collaborative demands were not factored into hiring, staffing, or evaluation metrics. As a result, managers reexamined job functions and role descriptions and reconsidered the internal cost allocations used to establish transfer pricing on IT projects.

Second, this view of collaborative effort helped determine where sufficient cross-role collaboration existed in order to capitalize on opportunities, and where it needed to be built up in order to avoid substantial costs. For example, before spending $200,000 on a larger server to solve a problem of slow response time, an application architect checked in with one of the infrastructure architects. It turned out that the slow response time was caused by a single query transaction that was initiating intensive database activity, so the right solution in this case was simply to change the database commands for the query transaction, which saved $200,000—a solution that would not have been discovered without effective collaboration between the infrastructure and application architects.

The CIO also identified a pattern of costly collaborative failures. She highlighted a breakdown in collaboration between infrastructure architects and application developers in a recent deployment of a network-intensive application. The development team had tested the application across a local area network but experienced substantial problems when extending the application to satellite offices with much lower network bandwidth. If the infrastructure architects had been involved early and often, they would have foreseen this problem; but at this late date, the solutions were either to increase bandwidth or to rewrite the application to reduce the network-intensiveness of transactions. The former solution can be prohibitively expensive for a far-flung network; the latter solution involved additional development, software licenses, and deployment costs—expenses that would have been avoided by early involvement of an infrastructure architect and simulation of application performance across the planned user community.

To avoid such scenarios in the future, the CIO used Table 4.1 to assess cross-role interaction costs and to determine where efficiencies could be realized or—as in the preceding example—where further investment of time across roles was warranted. This network view helped her to see that rather than simply allocating all costs to a given role or unit, it would be better to assign a cost to friction points that exist across roles. For example, compare the average costs of collaboration for the two roles with the largest number of employees—application architects and infrastructure architects. Application architects design and maintain major applications that support critical business processes or functions. They typically specialize in one or a small number of applications. Infrastructure architects help manage systemwide resources and are likely to be involved with a wide range of IT issues. Using a traditional budgeting process, management would likely consider the cost of both roles as similar types of stand-alone costs of the IT function. The network view highlights the important collaboration component of the costs of each role and gives management the opportunity to think of the costs and benefits of each role in conjunction with the likely impacts on other roles within IT or the entire organization.

This perspective can also be applied to assess the collaborative effectiveness of employees within a given role. For example, in this CIO's group, we assessed both time spent in interactions and value created by them. In this case, value was assessed in terms of the effectiveness that colleagues ascribed to information they received from others in the network. As shown in Figure 4.3, plotting these two relationships—time spent and information value—provides insight into those who are more effective in their role and who provide greater value for the time they consume. Although the figure shows that most employees fall within a fairly tight group, there are clearly outliers and opportunities for improvement (those who consume a lot of time and provide relatively little value), which informed coaching in this case.

Figure 4.3. Plotting Value Creation and Cost in Networks

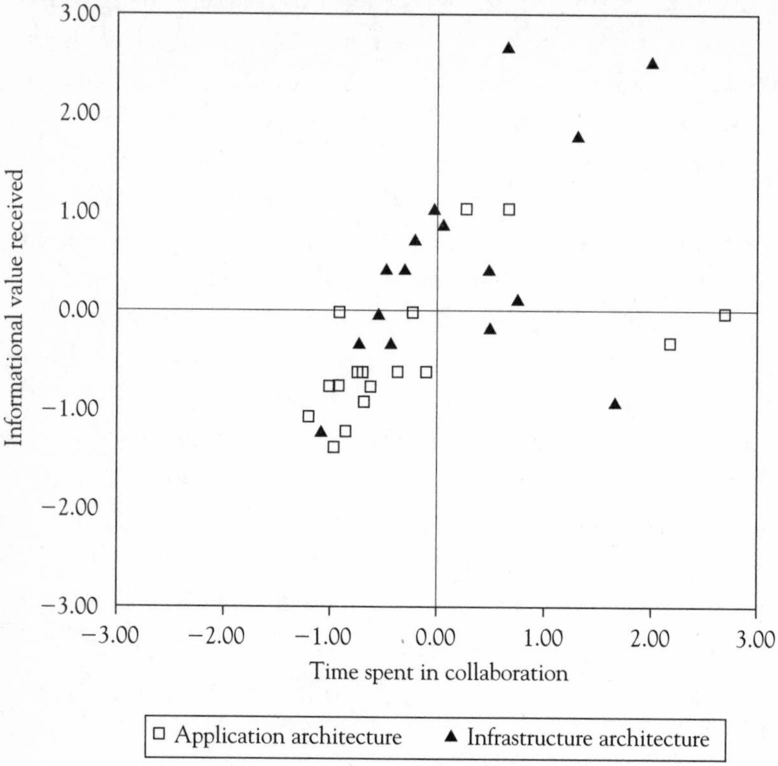

Conclusion

Because collaboration is an increasingly critical feature of organizational life and a major driver of value, revenue, and cost, leaders need to be able to peel back the layers of a network to identify the most promising opportunities for improvement. Instead of promoting overall connectivity—and thereby overwhelming employees and creating bottlenecks—leaders can use network analysis to make targeted investments in collaborative efforts with clear economic returns. They can replicate the network characteristics that deliver value, assess costs in an entirely new way, and develop more accurate understandings of people's productivity and role effectiveness.

In this chapter we have shown how, after examining value creation and cost with network analysis, leaders often develop very different ideas about how economic value is created throughout an organization. Applied in this way, network analysis can help by:

1. *Defining and replicating networks of high-performing individuals and teams.* Making networks that yield revenue visible enables leaders to create talent processes that build these networks more rapidly throughout an organization. This approach consistently yields substantial revenue impact in comparison to traditional interventions such as sales or product training.

2. *Revealing collaborations central to efficiency through measures of time or dollar savings resulting from collaborations within a network.* This view allows leaders to model anticipated financial return from network investments in technology, roles, or infrastructure and thus helps to inform where and how much to reasonably invest in collaboration.

3. *Assessing collaborations that enable revenue generation.* Measuring value creation in this way helps leaders to isolate points where they need to invest in order to more effectively bring expertise to important clients (for example, through targeted account management or cross-selling). It also ensures that those who enable others to be effective in sales efforts do not go unrecognized and consequently leave the organization (thereby dramatically but often invisibly affecting revenue production).

4. *Visualizing cost structures relationally in order to improve cultural tendencies, decision-right allocation, role design, and on occasion, individual employee effectiveness.* Most people in organizations spend more than three-quarters of their time in meetings, on phone calls, or corresponding via e-mail. It only makes sense that leaders begin to use network analysis to address the magnitude and drivers of these ballooning costs of collaboration.

5

DELIVERING RESULTS THROUGH PROCESS NETWORKS

It is common for us to be called into an organization after a reengineering or process redesign effort and to find ineffective collaboration offsetting efficiencies anticipated from work-flow improvements. Ours is not a unique vantage: a recent McKinsey survey of 7,827 executives found that nearly 80 percent of these executives rated their organization as "ineffective" at or "experiencing difficulty" with critical collaborations.[24] The problem is that traditional process mapping and improvement techniques too often miss inefficiencies driven by collaborative breakdowns in networks.

For example, we frequently see people who were effective in a prechange organization become overloaded in the restructured organization as both old and new colleagues consume their time. Such bottlenecks, which develop invisibly without an ONA, dramatically affect both morale and organizational performance in ways that process maps can neither locate nor remedy. Alternatively, we often see people removed from a network (either through headcount reduction or restaffing) as part of a process redesign without anyone realizing the critical impact these people, and sometimes even entire roles (such as middle managers), had in enabling others to be effective. The result can be substantial disruption to execution, problem solving, and innovation throughout an organization.

Of course, neither process improvement methodologies nor ONA work best alone. Process redesign or reengineering techniques focus on improving task effectiveness but often miss opportunities that network analysis can reveal, and network analysis alone can overemphasize relationships, to the detriment of locating task efficiencies. As work in general becomes increasingly collaborative, organizations will require methodologies that reflect the need to streamline processes while also recognizing performance improvement opportunities that can be derived through networks. In the remainder of this chapter we provide two cases—one on a decision-making process, the other on a core work process—to illustrate the power of combining network analysis and process improvement methods.

Improving Decision Processes with Network Analysis

In ten years, Cedarwood Pharmaceuticals[25] had grown from a five-person, single-product startup into a large, multidrug pharmaceutical company with more than three thousand employees. Senior management attributed Cedarwood's success to its culture of collaboration and inclusion. However, the CEO was concerned that the entrepreneurial culture that had made Cedarwood successful had become an obstacle to efficient and effective decision making. Decision-making processes were hampered by conflicting goals across functions. Nearly three-quarters of employees surveyed said they spent more than half of their time in meetings that lacked any set agenda and produced action items that were implemented less than 50 percent of the time.

To address the situation, the CEO tasked a multidivisional team with establishing an effective decision-making process that would empower employees as well as yield sound and timely decisions. The team's first step was to track a series of decisions as they made their way through the organization, recording the duration and ultimate result of each decision maker's involvement. Process maps built from this effort revealed substantial inefficiencies: decisions tended to involve too many people, to escalate too high in the organization, and to be revisited too many times throughout the process.

For example, one seemingly obvious capital-expenditure decision originated in a conversation among four directors but then required Herculean effort to get approved. The decision went on a five-month journey that reinvolved the four directors at several points and consumed the time of two lower-level managers, analysts who had to run numbers several times, a director in a third department, and two executives—all ultimately to approve a decision that had been amended only slightly from the original version. If the four directors had had even minimal capital-expenditure decision authority, the purchase would have been made months earlier and at a fraction of the labor and opportunity costs.

Unfortunately, this kind of inefficiency permeated Cedarwood in decisions ranging from pricing to hiring and promotion to even the most trivial travel approvals. The result was extremely high collaborative costs on even mundane approvals. One decision regarding a $39,000 purchase logged $17,000 in labor costs over two months. Another four-month decision, which involved twenty-five people in a single month, incurred direct labor costs of more than $60,000. And of course, labor costs reflect only a portion of the economic impact of inefficient decision processes. In pharmaceuticals, the opportunity cost of delayed new-product introduction is a substantial inefficiency (typically valued at $1 million per day) that can be traced to managers' having to occupy themselves with trivial or routine decisions rather than moving products through the pipeline.

The information flow network revealed a substantial degree of overcommunication compared to similar leadership networks in other organizations. To address the root causes of overinclusion, the team used the ONA to assess both time spent in decision-making interactions and the primary and secondary roles that colleagues played in those interactions: decision maker, input provider, advice provider, individual who wants to know, and individual who simply feels a need to know. Assessing time spent in decision making enabled the team to quantify the costs of overinclusion and isolate where costs could be taken out of the network. For example, as shown in Figure 5.1, 60 percent of the time that employees reported spending with colleagues on decision making was with colleagues they identified as either input or advice providers—yet most of these decisions did not require consensus at anywhere near that level. Similarly, substantial interactions were also driven to pacify people who "wanted to know" or felt they "needed to know"—a legacy of the organization's collaborative culture that could not be sustained.

The network analysis also helped identify routine decisions in which approval processes involved many more people than necessary. Results showed that the average employee at or above

Figure 5.1. Decision-Making Roles at Cedarwood

Number of hours employees reported spending with the following people:

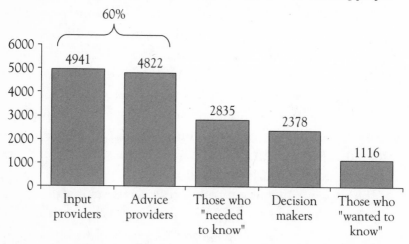

ONA questions: What roles do these people typically perform when involved in your decision-making processes? Please provide an estimate for the total number of hours you spend involved in decision making with these people in a typical month.

the level of manager involved thirteen people in his or her decision making each week, and nine of these people provided input or advice. By contrast, in comparable leadership networks, the average employee involved between five and seven colleagues in similar decision cycles. Simply paring back the network to meet this benchmark target reduced the average number of costly and time-consuming interactions by 33 percent on a monthly basis.

For example, the ONA and some interviews revealed that Cedarwood's legal department participated too frequently in routine and nonroutine decisions. Because of previous sanctions from the Food and Drug Administration over mistakes on new-product filings, the organization as a whole became excessively cautious and, as a result, included the legal department in practically all decisions. Ultimately, well-communicated guidelines issued by the legal department on a range of routine decisions helped to reduce its direct involvement in common decision-making interactions.

ONA also highlighted the inefficiencies caused by an overly hierarchical decision-making network—a result that truly surprised management, who believed the culture of Cedarwood to be egalitarian and empowering. When decision rights are not clear or well allocated, the tendency is for every decision to work its way up the hierarchy. This is exactly what happened at Cedarwood as managers at the level of vice president and above became bottlenecks in the decision-making process, working to their limits and still not meeting the vast number of decision requests. One vice president indicated that "it wasn't until I saw myself and my fellow VPs at the center of these networks that I realized just how reliant other positions were on us. I feel like I am making things happen all the time—but that really isn't true. It's just a bubble of activity around me and I was missing a lot of things on the edge of the network, where key innovations should be happening. I suddenly felt horrible about the stack of things on my desk and in my e-mail that I wasn't executing on and so holding up a tremendous amount of activity."

Figure 5.2 quantifies the impression given by this leader. Far more than any other position, senior leaders had become primary decision makers (and in many ways unintentional decision blockers) for employees at all levels. Decision-making authority was clearly concentrated in the hands of managers at or above the VP level, excessively consuming their time as well as that of managers forced to reach up the hierarchy.

Cedarwood's rapid organic growth had produced a lack of clarity on roles, responsibilities, authority, and empowerment. Consequently, leadership had become involved in too many decisions, which resulted in a hierarchical network despite egalitarian and inclusive values. Believing that they were only being thorough, leaders quizzed and challenged employees about the most basic details of their assumptions and often told them to run the numbers a different way. Employees often felt chastised and were left with the impression that they could not and should not make independent decisions—especially because they would be subjected to scrutiny and, all too often, reversal.

Figure 5.2. Reliance on Managerial Levels for Decision Making at Cedarwood

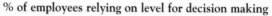

% of employees relying on level for decision making

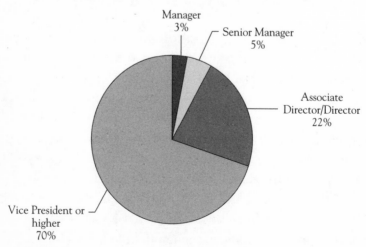

Of course, most leaders in the central positions did not really experience problems with decision making because they got to make, or were in the loop on, all decisions that mattered to them. As a result, the biggest challenge for the team at Cedarwood was to convince leaders that concentrating decision making at the VP level was not a sustainable or effective means of doing business. By quantifying the economic impact of impractical decision making, the network results made it very clear that senior leaders desperately needed to distance themselves from some decisions while empowering others to own decisions and develop future leaders.

Because the ONA asked the survey participants to estimate (and validate through examples) the number of hours they spent in decision making with other individuals, we could quantify the economic impact of impractical decision-making processes. Aggregating and converting time spent into interaction costs (by multiplying time in collaborations against loaded compensation figures) allowed the team to show that each month Cedarwood's management consumed 17,400 hours of people's network time on decision making, incurring labor costs that totaled a staggering $1.4 million. We also quantified cost savings associated with paring back the most unnecessary collaborations in the decision-making process and found that the amount of time employees reported spending with those they identified as input or advice providers cost the company nearly $800,000 in labor costs each month—more than half of the total cost of collaborations across all decision making.

Cedarwood ultimately implemented an enterprisewide program composed of three major initiatives that sped execution and removed inefficiencies from decision-making networks. First, the team drafted guides on overall decision-making principles and practices, and produced decision-flow models for the most common and important decision types. By decreasing the density of the decision-making network and effectively delegating and communicating routine decision roles and rights, the number of costly and time-consuming interactions with extraneous roles—such as those who "wanted to know"—was dramatically cut. For example, decisions on pricing and distribution associated with an upgraded product were commonly considered by two separate committees—one for pricing and one for distribution. The two groups were integrated into a single team, reduced in size, and given broader decision-making authority so that proposals would not need to be circulated through the network.

Second, senior leadership established a steering committee to reconsider governance principles and practices. The goal of this initiative was to ensure that employees knew how and why they were to take responsibility for their own decisions and that they could easily understand the structure of accountability within the organization. One key output of this group was to reduce the numbers and sizes of committees quickly and dramatically so that fewer people were involved in decisions and so that those who were involved in core strategic initiatives were held accountable for being more timely and decisive. The combined pricing and distribution committee, for example, was given an explicit mandate to move faster. In addition, the committee instituted meeting-management practices so that remaining meetings would run more smoothly.

Third, the CEO instituted a cultural and behavioral change program that involved leadership and conflict resolution training. The goal of this initiative was to reinforce individual accountability as well as to reduce the cost of inclusion and the sense of entitlement that people felt about being consulted on even trivial decisions. Conflict resolution training was instituted to ensure that where ambiguities existed, decisions could keep moving without generating frustration or hostility. To evaluate the success of this additional training, the company added decision-making proficiency to the key personal competencies examined in performance evaluations. Leaders were evaluated on how well they adhered to their assigned roles in routine decisions, as well as on the extent to which they helped minimize the time and interactions involved in routine decisions.

These three initiatives were celebrated by the company's employees, who saw them as the first steps toward rekindling Cedarwood's egalitarian culture. Senior leaders were also thrilled because they had previously worried that growth would cancel a strong and attractive culture of collaboration. They knew now that collaboration could survive, even as the organization grew in size and complexity. The president indicated that "in the end, the project was a huge success based on savings generated on a handful of decisions—not to mention the impact on the organization's culture and behavior. It's also going to prove invaluable as we prepare for aggressive growth in the near future."

Improving Core Work Processes with Network Analysis[*]

The Jupiter Company[26] is a multibillion-dollar food organization that was struggling with the complexity and cross-functional nature of several core work processes. Because revenue growth in mature products had slowed, senior management decided to improve bottom-line results by making these processes more efficient. As part of this initiative, management appointed process owners, who were charged with finding ways to cut costs, boost efficiency, and improve the consistency of operations.

The packaging design process faced particularly daunting challenges. This workflow is crucial because it creates attractive packaging that will capture consumers' attention and because it is a time-sensitive activity: to remain competitive, the packaging design process must be highly efficient so that products can be brought to market quickly and inexpensively. Unfortunately, it is also a highly complex, cross-functional process requiring a variety

---

[*]*Note:* We are extremely thankful to Jean Singer and John Helferich for bringing this case to our attention.

of roles to work together fluidly—from brand managers, who conceive of a new product and its appearance; to packaging experts, who convert concepts into precise specifications of materials; to graphic designers, who create artwork; to financial analysts, who compile cost information and determine margins; to external suppliers, who provide materials; and finally to process leaders, who help coordinate the roles and functions involved. Collaboration is essential because all roles are highly interdependent in terms of information that needs to be shared, task execution that needs to be synchronized, and ideas that need to coalesce into innovative packaging designs.

Over time, Jupiter had begun to see signs that the packaging design process was in trouble. Error rates on packaging specifications had steadily increased to around 15 percent, which was not only undermining customers' confidence but also costing the company millions of dollars. These errors also had an effect on performance in that employees became so overwhelmed by the demands of both correcting errors and executing the process that they had little or no time to generate new packaging ideas that could fuel growth. It was clear that the packaging design team needed to find ways to reduce error rates dramatically while streamlining the process and reducing labor and error-related inefficiencies.

To address these issues, the team applied process mapping and activity analysis. Process participants were interviewed extensively to create *As Is* maps that described the steps in the packaging design process. These diagrams were analyzed and converted into *To Be* maps that depicted how the process ideally should operate. The team then used these maps, in conjunction with some automation, to make rote activities less labor intensive, to provide more timely access to accurate data, and to streamline work activities and documentation across a number of steps. For example, an SAP system was implemented that housed data on product weight so that people in design, production, and financial roles could all have access to the same figures at the touch of a keystroke. Thanks to process-wide automation and streamlined documentation, employees were able to carry out their individual tasks more proficiently.

Yet despite some wins, management had clear evidence that the process improvement approach had not generated the entire range of possible efficiencies. Rather than make a single pass through design, costing, and production approvals, a design would "churn," circulating through the three roles in a seemingly endless loop. This process caused frustration among employees in their dealings with colleagues in other roles and began to impact morale and turnover. A survey of process participants showed that 49 percent felt that the packaging design process was good to excellent in effectiveness (the ability to produce high-quality outcomes), but only 25 percent felt the same about efficiency (the ability to get things done quickly, without a lot of waiting or waste). A whopping 49 percent felt that process efficiency was poor.

People got the job done, but at an extraordinarily high cost in terms of time and effort. An ONA of the packaging design process revealed four critical inefficiencies. First, the volume of collaborations in the network was almost twice the number expected, clearly signaling that the process was operating in relational overload. People had created a far more complex web of interactions than the process required. These excessive interactions detracted from efficiency as people worked with those colleagues they wanted to work with and engaged in numerous work-arounds to complete their tasks. Because there had been no formal process training or official manual for packaging design, employees had invented their own ways of working, with each person finding the routes that he or she felt were best and creating a variety of networks for any given role.

After seeing the network diagrams, one manager noted, "The process is done multiple different ways, and everyone keeps their process to themselves." For example, each materials technician used a different network for ordering and receiving packaging materials, with the only shared contact being the packaging supplier. With an assortment of personalized approaches, no single practice or process was fully optimized, and a lack of shared expectations led to substantial confusion and conflict.

A second discovery became evident after weighing each of the roles for their centrality—that is, the number of ties each role had to others in the process. A high level of centrality means that the people in that role are situated in the middle of handoffs and as a result can either expedite or block the process. Whereas process maps contain information on the participation of different roles, the interactions are hidden among dozens of task boxes. The network view brings this information to the forefront so that management can see at a glance which roles are highly influential.

The ONA for packaging design showed that two vendors, the packaging supplier and the graphics supplier, connected with roughly two-thirds of the roles. Contracting with these vendors in a way that forged strong working relationships with consistent interactions suddenly emerged as much more important than haggling over each job's individual cost. The packaging design team realized it needed to look beyond contractual arrangements and focus on ways to vest these important external partners in the process to the fullest degree. For example, they began to include the vendors in activities such as process training and team building, and they consulted with them as equal partners on process-design issues.

Third, the network view enabled the team not just to see where people were interacting in the packaging design process, but also to evaluate the quality of those interactions. In this case, it turned out that marketing, a key role in packaging design, had poor-quality interactions with six different roles. For example, the packaging coordinators depended on the marketing staff for estimates of timing and volume so they could schedule equipment with plant personnel. Alternatively, the commercial graphics staff needed to achieve consensus between marketing staff and graphic designers. Unfortunately, instead of engaging with the various roles productively and rising to its central function in the process, marketing was a bottleneck, driving slowness and confusion across roles. This discovery led to role redesign and the institution of an educational program to help marketing personnel become versed in the process and their role within it.

Finally, one of the most striking discoveries from the network analysis had to do with the amount of people-related change that would be required to implement process improvements. Management's original assumption, based on process maps, was that the majority of changes had to do with automation, which they could implement simply by training employees on the new computer system. In their minds, this was confirmed by a comparison of the As Is and To Be process maps—few things had changed that weren't driven by automation.

However, the process maps didn't uncover the complexity of the roles. In contrast, the network analysis revealed that there were major differences between the actual activities and those depicted in either the As Is or the To Be process maps. For example, the process maps indicated that the margin analysts had to interact only with accounting personnel. These maps were a far cry from the real world of the margin analyst, who, according to the network analysis, operated in a complex web of interactions with ten other roles to gather and confirm data on costs and pricing. To make the transition to a new mode of operating, the margin analysts needed to shift behaviors, to abandon networks that were no longer necessary, and to retain those they would need in order to work in conjunction with the new computer system.

Overall, the effort showed that, as a tool, the process maps were limited in their ability to convey variability or the full complexity of roles. A network analysis can more accurately capture the intricacies of working relationships and more fully describe the differences between actual and desired behavior. Furthermore, we were able to take these descriptions down to each role in the process and highlight the five roles that would undergo the greatest change. In each case, the ONA illustrated the relational changes that needed to take place for that role to be effective in the new environment, which enabled management to train people on the old ties they needed to reevaluate as well as on the new ones they needed to build.

Conclusion

Too often, redesign efforts underdeliver when traditional approaches to process improvement do not allow managers to see informal networks and their impact. Process mapping is a highly effective tool in identifying inefficiencies through a linear view of how and where value is added to a service, product, or decision. Yet by its nature it often misses critical collaborations that are key to performance improvement in work that is recursive, knowledge-intensive, and nonroutine. In these kinds of work—which comprise the bulk of value-added activities in most organizations today—the result of taking only a process-based view is often a restructuring that dramatically disrupts networks and, ultimately, organizational performance.

As outlined in this chapter, combining process mapping and network analysis increases the odds of realizing efficiencies anticipated in reengineering and process redesign efforts. Specifically, leaders can derive substantial benefit by focusing this combined lens on decision making and core work processes.

Decision-making processes are often ineffective and substantial drivers of inefficiency in a range of organizations (from those experiencing rapid growth while clinging to informal processes or consensus-oriented cultures, to bureaucratic organizations caught in political gridlock or burdened by overly prescribed roles and procedures). Process maps can provide insights into points where value is or is not added as a decision works its way through an organization. ONA complements this view by enabling leaders to assess and put a cost to the myriad and often invisible interactions required to execute a decision. Minimizing non-value-added interactions as well as taking routine decisions (such as travel approvals and simple pricing decisions) out of the network improves execution and yields substantial cost savings in decision making.

Core work and innovation processes are also key points of value creation in flows that spread laterally throughout an organization. Complementing process maps with network analyses of information and decision-making interactions can more accurately capture the intricacies of working relationships and indicate where process maps are overly simplified. In this context, network analysis helps to identify where processes are ineffective due to given roles using multiple networks, where overly influential roles are dramatically affecting the quality and efficiency of others, and where relational changes need to take place for a role to be effective in the restructured environment.

6

DELIVERING RESULTS THROUGH PROJECT-BASED NETWORKS

Although teams appear to be an easy solution for leaders to apply to projects, too often ad hoc or large-scale implementation of teams creates hidden and excessive costs of collaboration, lengthy decision cycles, and diffusion of effort and focus.[27] A fundamental problem is that most organizations follow advice on team effectiveness from fifteen or so years ago, when people had the luxury of being able to commit their efforts to one team. With sufficient time to focus on team development activities, following traditional advice on team formation,[28] leadership and roles,[29] group process,[30] and organizational design[31] can yield effective groups. Unfortunately, this reality no longer exists. Teams today are formed and disbanded rapidly, distributed across multiple sites, and composed of members working simultaneously on several projects with different bosses competing for their attention—all while trying to deliver work products that require coordination of unique and highly specialized expertise.

Despite the frequency with which teams are dispatched to address important issues, most leaders, when pushed, readily acknowledge that teams are in fact *not* the primary vehicles by which results are produced in their organization. Reflect on your own experience for a moment. All of us have been on teams or committees where some colleagues drove substantial progress while others—sometimes even the leaders themselves—didn't really have the expertise, influence, or motivation to make things happen. Rather than high performance resulting from harmonious teams of equally contributing members, most projects and processes are enabled by productive networks that form among some (but not all) team members in combination with relationships that bridge to key resources and expertise outside of the team.

If they could look into their organizations and see these networks within and across key initiatives, most leaders would manage work differently. They might free up time for employees who turn out to be crucial to a given team's progress, and reassign those who do not contribute much to the effort. Or they might urge the team to listen to those who have become marginalized but whose perspective or expertise would help the team avoid downstream problems. Shifting from efforts that create cohesive teams to ones that enable rapid formation and dissolution of networks can greatly increase an organization's ability to drive performance at key points of execution deep within the organization.

Delivering Results Through Networks in Sales, Innovation, and Execution Teams

In project-based work such as professional services, research and development, software, and health care, an effective way to improve performance is to establish processes that replicate the networks of high-performing teams. For example, after conducting a network analysis in a global high-tech company across almost two hundred process-improvement and product-development teams, we found that the most innovative teams with on-time performance tended to share the following network characteristics: collaborations between the right roles at relevant points in a project, lateral connectivity across team members, lack of hierarchical information seeking, and diverse ties to relevant parties both inside and outside the organization. Embedding practices that helped newly appointed team leaders build these networks more rapidly and naturally throughout dozens of teams in the organization had a substantial impact on the efficiency and yield of these projects.

In our work across various kinds of organizations, we have seen network analysis produce substantial results in three prevalent types of teams: sales, innovation, and execution. Each type of team has a unique set of network characteristics that most commonly yields performance improvement opportunities.

Sales Teams

Since the 1980s, many industrial and professional services organizations have implemented account team structures to serve key clients. Yet traditional account team structures and account planning practices have somehow not matched the complexity of identifying and exploiting emerging opportunities in the highest-potential accounts. In fact, research has shown no correlation between the use of teams and sales performance on key accounts.[32] The difference between high- and low-performing account teams is not a result of product knowledge, sales behaviors, or more traditional account-planning practices. In most organizations, key-account teams have the same training and access to the same technologies. As a result, team-building or sales-training interventions often pale in comparison to the improvement potential uncovered by addressing the following three network drivers of account team success:

Quality of relationships between the account team and the client.
The appropriate level of high-quality client connections between team members and a key account allows for better client service, discovery of selling opportunities, and decreased susceptibility to the departure of important individuals on both sides of the relationship.

Quality of relationships within the account team. A team that fluidly connects expertise and roles is much more efficient and effective in identifying and capitalizing on sales and delivery opportunities than teams that don't.

Quality of relationships connecting the team with the host orga-nization. A broad network of connections back into the organization allows an account team to leverage an orga-nization's scale and thus materialize the right products, services, and expertise for clients in a timely and efficient fashion.

A global information technology services company we worked with delivered significant outsourcing and consulting projects through client service teams of one hundred or more employees. This company had assigned account teams to its top clients—each of which accounted for 2 to 7 percent of total revenue—with the mission of improving customer retention and driving revenue growth. Given the substantial revenue implica-tions of these accounts, senior management was keenly inter-ested in narrowing the performance gap between the high- and low-revenue-generating teams. A network analysis across these accounts revealed how high-performing teams' networks—and low-performing teams' lack of networks—affected revenue generation.

Although changes were most obvious and significant among the low-performing accounts, many senior leaders were surprised by the degree to which even the high-performing teams ben-efited from this program. For example, one account team that serviced a leading wealth-management company conducted the network analysis to strengthen an already healthy relationship. The account executive's primary goals were to improve coordi-nation within the team and to establish the right connections with the client across dimensions such as seniority, roles, func-tions, and expertise.

The ONA revealed a number of opportunities at both the team and individual team member levels. Here we focus on just three points that highlight how a network perspective can improve effectiveness in large, distributed account teams where traditional advice on teams does not work and best-practice program manage-ment methodologies create overly rigid groups that do not morph to meet clients' needs. First, the account manager was astonished by how many team members, at all levels, had relationships with multiple employees at the client organization. We often find account team performance suffering because lack of connectivity with a client undermines the ability to sell holistic solutions and makes the team highly susceptible when decision makers change roles or leave the client organization. In this case, the account executive found the reverse—that excessive, uncoordinated communication was creating confusion on key sales efforts and service delivery. He quickly implemented a communication strategy and account contact plan to ensure that everyone was aligned with the client's objectives and delivering a consistent message.

Second, looking at the network from a different perspective revealed the external and internal focus of various people on the team. Some team members were boundary spanners, holding subgroups together—in this case, the IT services team held critical relationships with the client. On the IT team, the spanners were the desktop technicians who provided VIP support to key client stakeholders. They were influential with the client in ways that the account executive had never realized. As a result, changes were made in account planning to leverage these people for additional insights on sales opportunities and political dynamics in the client's organization.

A third point of interest for the account executive lay with identifying the people on his team whom most other teammates relied on and who held the deepest relationships with the key people at the client organization. "It was clear that our incentives rewarded a hero mentality. Individual account personnel could excel financially by controlling the account. Of course this had all sorts of limitations to it, with turnover, lack of account penetration, and sometimes poor service. Using these results to profile the high-performing teams and then sharing these profiles with less successful account executives provided an immediate change in how those accounts were working," the account executive indicated.

Among his team's overly connected members was a woman named Sue who was about to go on a leave of absence. The ONA allowed the account executive to zoom in on Sue to understand her relationships so that he could avoid disruption while she was away. Some of Sue's relationships were also held by other senior account personnel. It turned out, however, that Sue was the primary point of contact for many key decision makers at the client. For those contacts with whom she held the sole relationship, she immediately began teaming with another person to build the relationship before she left. Because several of the other senior account personnel were overloaded, the account manager decided to pair Sue with "high-potential" team members who were ready to take on client responsibilities.

In addition to taking such targeted actions on a team-by-team basis, understanding what the high-performing teams were doing through their networks enabled this company to embed network-centric practices across all account teams. All account executives began to use the network analysis results in account planning to help ensure that their teams were building appropriate connections with clients, coordinating well internally, reaching out appropriately to the organization to leverage specialized expertise, and not becoming overly reliant on a subset of leaders or experts. Shifts in sales-call protocols and account reports focused and measured efforts on network-building activities that immediately increased client penetration across a number of these teams.

A new collaborative technology (which the teams were required to use) also had an immediate impact on the breadth of sales as members of various teams shared tips and information about offerings. Importantly, this technology was designed to help people find the skills and experiences of those in other accounts whom they could leverage for their own needs, and was also very effective in coordinating efforts via collaborative forums created for each account. As a result, the technology naturally supported the network that needed to form around key clients rather than simply adding another collaborative demand.

Finally, personal network profiles were leveraged to give feedback on individual team members' networks and, through a benchmarking process, to show how each employee's networks compared with other networks. These profiles helped account leaders and team members develop connections that both benefited the team and advanced the team members' careers.

Innovation Teams

Innovation success often comes from targeted initiatives that ensure connectivity among those with the right expertise in a given domain and those with the right influence in the organization—the people who can get things done by virtue of their position in the network. Rather than sequestering small teams with a charge to generate a blinding insight or engaging in yet another corporate restructuring to break down silos, leaders can use ONA to mobilize networks of relevant expertise. Networks can improve innovation success by

1. *Staffing innovation teams with brokers from broader informational networks.* By mapping networks of groups charged with innovation (such as R&D units or learning-oriented alliances), organizations can staff innovation teams with brokers—those well positioned to see the potential of an idea from one domain for application in another—and greatly facilitate integration of expertise in breakthrough innovations.

2. *Developing targeted external ties for decision making.* Obtaining buy-in and decision acceptance from both formal and informal leaders in the broader organizational network dramatically improves the speed and fidelity of execution as an innovation evolves from ideation to implementation.

3. *Recombining existing expertise and resources to produce innovation breakthroughs.* Mapping the quality of ties among those

with core expertise ensures that the right combinations of knowledge and resources are integrating to generate new product or service offerings.

The My M&M's business of MasterFoods—the group that developed and now markets customized M&M's—provides an example of how mobilizing internal and external networks can result in such breakthrough innovations. The spark for the new business occurred in the advanced technology team in R&D, which was charged with developing new technologies for the Chocolate Business Unit. Inspired by the legendary *m* printed on M&M's, the team was intrigued by the opportunity to create a new appearance for the candy. The first innovation came with learning how to "ink-jet" a picture onto a tablet of chocolate, which led to the development of a food-grade system to print digital photos directly onto the surface of a chocolate bar. However, although a technical success, beta testing with consumers did not show enough volume to justify launching the new M&M with customizable pictures on a large scale.

At the same time, another group within the same unit was charged with printing the faces of the M&M characters onto M&M's using offset lithographic technology. This technology is traditionally used to print onto confections, but not to the level of resolution required to print high-quality images onto the curved M&M surface. In this case, the market tests showed high interest in the product, but the cost of creating new print wheels prohibited small runs and precluded introducing the product.

Each team had an incremental success that was not viable in the market; but their combined insights had the potential to generate a substantial breakthrough. Although they were colocated at that time, the two groups did not communicate in a way that allowed them to see the connection between the new technology and the opportunity to print different logos on M&M's. The catalyst was a manager familiar with both groups—in network terms, a broker—who brought the two groups together by "translating" how the technology innovation could be applied to printing onto M&M's. Together the groups had an "ah-ha" moment, with the realization that the ink-jet technology from chocolate tablet printing could be combined with the concept of printing on M&M's. This collaboration created the ability to print text on M&M's at low volumes, allowing the company to cheaply customize the print on the M&M's piece and create the innovative business concept of selling custom-printed M&M's directly to consumers.

The groups now had to figure out how to execute this idea. They realized that several other networks needed to be built. The development team needed an external network of suppliers to provide key elements of technology, which resulted in the formation of an external partnership network composed of an ink-jet print-head supplier, an ink company, and a printer frame fabricator. Next, the team built a network within MasterFoods by systematically reaching out to those in other functional groups who would be critical in moving the technical innovation from prototype to market.

Finally, buy-in from management was needed. Luckily the MasterFoods management team was looking for a new venture that could serve as an example of business model innovation for the rest of the firm, and this project fit in perfectly. Although My M&M's promised high profit potential, resistance came from among the company's leaders, who saw in the new business a completely unfamiliar financial model. To facilitate buy-in, the executive sponsor of the venture reached out to the personal network he had created with the finance leadership to get acceptance and specifically asked them to lead beta teams throughout the enterprise in testing the new business model internally. This creative collaboration helped break down internal barriers and enabled the beta test of the new business to be implemented in sixty days, a breathtaking improvement over the normal two-and-a-half years for new-product introduction.

Execution Teams

Execution teams such as project teams in professional services, software development teams in technology, and service teams in a range of industries generate value through the creation and delivery of services. Their success in executing on time and within budget depends on effective and efficient coordination.[33] In most cases, coordination issues are addressed by developing and applying a process map that governs how work will be done across individual roles and responsibilities. Yet process maps alone do not enable the informal collaboration that is necessary for coordination and are often inflexible when it comes to exceptions or unexpected changes. By adding a network perspective, execution teams can find new opportunities for improvement on the following key network dimensions:

1. *Building mutual awareness of current work and expertise.* Greater awareness of skills and expertise helps in execution and informs members of colleagues' work, thereby speeding coordination of effort.

2. *Forming cohesive, specialized subgroups knit together by technical brokers.* Large execution teams break into largely autonomous subgroups to focus on specialized work. In these cases, broker roles evolve and are critical to bridging subteams to allow for efficient execution and then integration of highly specialized work.

3. *Leveraging external relationships for product and service adaptation.* External ties provide independent evaluation and calibration of the work in order to improve acceptance of the product and customers' satisfaction with it.

Effective networks are especially important for software development teams, which need to build a single, coherent system whose parts fit together seamlessly. Software development processes are complex. Although work is often done in multiple locations, the overall structure of the software is handled through a high-level design and architecture agreement and sometimes by a governance structure. Given this complexity, it is not surprising that software development teams often turn in poor performance, resulting in costly rework, reduced quality, and lower customer satisfaction. However, in one technology company we observed three teams that used a network lens along with common software development processes and tools to deliver their projects on time, on budget, and with a high level of both client and team satisfaction. Several network factors were critical to these teams' success.

In large software-development teams composed of people with disparate expertise, team members are often unaware of the knowledge and skills of others on their team. The ONA from the teams we studied (which ranged in size from 23 to 83 members) revealed that team members were aware of the knowledge and skills of approximately 56 percent of their teammates and aware of what approximately 50 percent of their teammates were working on. This level of awareness meant that people already had knowledge of where to find the right expertise within the team and could coordinate their work more easily than by relying on written documentation, which is often out-of-date and incomplete.

This high level of awareness was aided by the fact that several people on each team had previously worked together and therefore were familiar with one another's knowledge and skills. These teams, however, also went out of their way to raise awareness by arranging face-to-face rather than virtual meetings and by using communication technologies, especially instant messaging, which promoted both local and remote collaboration.

Although many teams make the mistake of increasing communication without thinking through who really needs to be involved in decisions, two of the software teams in this organization used the ONA to divide into small subgroups based on core tasks and expertise and set up appropriate communication between them. This structure allowed them to complete a lot of work simultaneously and meet some aggressive deadlines. When it comes to staffing, many managers focus on acquiring people who have the best skills for the project, forgetting that knowledge is just as often acquired from people outside of the team. What these successful teams did was encourage individuals with strong ties to go outside the team to get important technical information and feedback. There were a few reasons for this: to augment internal knowledge or canvas a wide range of people for information, to get specific technical information and help related to programming rather than general information, and to avoid the embarrassment of revealing ignorance to their teammates.

Management of these teams also played a factor in their success. The project managers of one of the teams arranged for the developers, who were geographically dispersed, to visit the client, who was in another country, in order to witness the project requirements firsthand and develop a stronger relationship with and allegiance to the client. To further strengthen that commitment, the project managers also arranged for members of the client team to visit the developers at their sites. These face-to-face meetings had a profound effect on clarifying the context of the requirements and created a level of trust that resulted in much richer and more productive communications and on-time delivery of the software.

Rapidly Forming Networks at the Point of Execution

As the preceding examples make clear, a network perspective reveals a number of important relational drivers of performance that traditional team-building efforts miss. By focusing on the right sets of both internal and external ties, this perspective gives leaders a much more detailed means of promoting team effectiveness. Table 6.1 outlines six questions that can help team leaders improve the effectiveness of their teams by attending to key network levers.

Table 6.1.   The Changing Face of Teams

Team Levers	Old View	New View
Are the right voices influencing the team trajectory?	The leader is the ultimate decision maker and direction setter. Process and content roles in the team provide structure.	Decision making and direction setting influence shifts based on expertise. Leader and followers set climate for shifts in responsibility.
Is the team appropriately connected for the task at hand?	Information and decision-making networks are either overconnected or hierarchical.	Information and decision-making networks are focused on an archetype for success based on point in process.
Has the team cultivated important external relationships?	External connectivity is not heavily emphasized either to others within the organization or to experts outside the organization.	External connectivity is heavily emphasized and targeted both within and outside the organization to bring the best expertise to bear.
Are value-added collaborations occurring in the team network?	Principal focus is on information and decision-making interactions.	Focus is on value-added interactions in terms of both performance and team members' engagement.
Do underlying relationship qualities yield effective collaboration?	Focus is on communication through joint commitment to goals, benevolence-based trust, and group process and harmony.	Focus is expanded to consider awareness of expertise, timely accessibility, competence-based trust, and execution of commitments made to teammates.
Does the organizational context support effective collaboration?	Emphasis is on matrix reporting structures, 360-degree performance feedback, team-based collaborative technologies, and flexible organizational affiliation.	Emphasis is on positive organizational network momentum, supported by consistent meaningful exposure to others' expertise, organization-wide collaborative technologies, and flexible work flow.

Question 1: Are the Right Voices Influencing the Team's Trajectory?

Traditional team-building advice suggests that high performance is the result of combining the right expertise with strong leadership and well-defined process and content roles.[34] With sufficient time and predictable problem domains, leaders can cultivate and gain commitment to a shared vision and match roles and accountabilities with team members' expertise. Of course, few team leaders have the luxury of this kind of time anymore. Most are dealing with nebulous problems and may not even know who will be on or off the team in coming weeks and months. So instead of designing a vision, process, and structure for a known future, team leaders must instead ensure that the right expertise is being brought to bear at the right moment—a difficult challenge with large, virtual, cross-functional teams too often staffed with members not dedicated to one effort.[35]

There are two things leaders must do to best utilize expertise on the team. First, they must ensure that the right expertise is influential and being called on. Too often certain voices—typically those that are loud, have the leader's ear, or have expertise that was good for past purposes—become too prominent in team collaborations and decision making. Cliques can also form and preclude the integration of important expertise, creating an invisible barrier to innovation and execution that the team was formed to bridge in the first place. In these cases, mapping information flow and problem-solving collaborations and then coloring nodes in the network according to technical competencies allows a leader to identify the most relevant experts and ensure that they are influential in ideation and execution.

Second, it is equally critical that leaders ensure the right balance of reliance on formal structure (to ensure consistency and efficiency) and networks (to ensure innovation). Although climate or team development surveys can indicate that a team has become too rigid or hierarchical, these assessments offer little valuable advice on what to do. Network analysis lets a leader see where a team is relying too heavily on roles—whether on the team leader or on others—and so creating bottlenecks and potentially not leveraging the best expertise.

Question 2: Is the Team Appropriately Connected for the Task at Hand?

Although team leaders acknowledge the importance of collaboration, the tendency too often is to take either a more-is-better or an ad hoc approach to communication. Each philosophy can create unproductive network patterns. First, one of the unfortunate legacies of the advice industry that has built up around teams is a heavy emphasis on consensus and participative leadership. But decision making can slow to a crawl if the process requires participation from lots of stakeholders and excessive consensus. A network perspective lets leaders see time spent in collaborations in order to assess where excessive collaboration is interfering with a team's effectiveness.

A less systematic, ad hoc approach to collaboration can be just as problematic. Research over the past twenty years has consistently shown that people who make targeted investments in relationships perform better than those who simply build ever-larger networks.[36] The same general results apply to teams as well.[37] Unfortunately, however, most team leaders do little to build the right patterns of connectivity and thus allow team networks to fall into collaborations constrained by formal structure,[38] demographic similarity (or homophily),[39] and personality.[40] Although leaders cannot make people become friends, they can use network information to change staffing, team meetings, and a range of communication vehicles to ensure that homophily, organizational pressures, and inertia do not drive teams into biased or ineffective networks.

Network analysis helps to ensure that the right collaborations are occurring rather than allowing overly connected or ad hoc networks to evolve. To build only appropriate connections, leaders (often in conjunction with the team) first identify the ideal network that needs to be in place at a given point in a team's lifecycle. Then, by comparing existing collaborative patterns to the desired network, they can both build out needed relationships and decrease time spent on unproductive ones. The ideal network can be identified in several ways: In smaller teams, a leader can run an exercise to brainstorm the network that needs to be in place; in larger or distributed groups, a leader can embed survey questions into a network diagnostic tool to identify the ideal pattern; and more systematically—as some pharmaceutical and electronics companies have done in their new-product-development efforts—organizations can profile high-performing team networks at key points in a process and then provide teams with an archetype for success.

Question 3: Has the Team Cultivated Important External Relationships?

Another legacy of the team-building advice industry is the inward-focused nature of the suggestions for teams, which too often promotes team insularity. Although most leaders intuitively know that there are useful ideas and practices outside the team, far too often teams draw only on their members' personal relationships for new ideas and expertise. Such lack of systematic attention to outside connections can be a problem when it comes to implementing a new idea, because the right partners can dramatically speed execution and time to market.

Network analysis can shift a team leader's focus to important external ties through an outside-in process. For example, in the traditional view of key account management, an account manager acts as a central coordinator of an account team that often comprises specialists representing various products, services, or divisions across the organization. When applying a network view to this same account, however, the team can see new opportunities and ensure that appropriate resources across the entire organization are accessed.

Question 4: Are Value-Added Collaborations Occurring in the Team Network?

Traditional team advice focuses on building commitment to a goal and then relies on roles, process, and structured meetings to ensure that information flow and decision making are occurring as required. Unfortunately, the tendency is to believe that more communication is better, but there is rarely any focus on the quality of the information or knowledge moving in the team. What we have seen time and again is that teams don't require lots of collaborative interactions; to meet their goals, they need only those collaborations that add value.

Using ONA, leaders can see where shifts in decision rights, accountabilities, and meeting formats can move a team from costly gridlock to execution. To get value-adding collaborations, leaders need to ask two questions: *Where have collaborations yielded value through best-practice transfer or knowledge sharing?* and *What collaborations drive revenue growth and can be replicated at certain points to generate greater value?*

Yet beyond ensuring that interactions are economically valuable, team leaders obtain tremendous traction by understanding how more-subjective interactions can disengage people from a team's goals and objectives. For example, by asking a simple question about energy in the network—*When you interact with this person, how does it affect your energy level (positive, neutral, or negative)?*—leaders can find the people who are capturing the hearts and minds of the team, those who are becoming less engaged, and those who may unintentionally be having a negative impact by virtue of how they interact with the group.

Question 5: Do Underlying Relationship Qualities Yield Effective Collaboration at the Point of Need?

Many of us have heard about, or participated in, team-building exercises such as ropes courses and falling backward into a teammate's arms. These activities may help forge friendships, but we have little evidence of how they improve collaboration. Teammates can be useful to one another only if two relational characteristics exist: an awareness of teammates' expertise and trust in their abilities.

If members of a team don't know what skills and expertise reside in the team—who knows what and who knows who knows what—the group as a whole will have a hard time leveraging the right expertise for a given problem or opportunity, or knowing which voices to listen to.[41] Once leaders spot this gap in awareness, they can take action, such as putting certain people together on key tasks, running meetings in ways that profile key expertise and challenges, and creating persona books or using other means of making team members' skills and resources visible.

People also need to know which colleagues they can trust. Research shows that trust leads to increased overall knowledge exchange,[42] makes knowledge exchange less costly,[43] and increases the likelihood that knowledge acquired from a colleague will be sufficiently understood and absorbed to be put to use.[44] Two dimensions of trust are important to knowledge creation and sharing on teams: benevolence ("You care about me and take an interest in my well-being and goals") and competence ("You have relevant expertise and can be depended on to know what you are talking about").[45] Benevolence-based trust, which is the goal of most traditional team-building activities, is important because it allows people to reveal their lack of knowledge to one another without fear. But people must also trust that the colleague they turn to is competent and has sufficient expertise to offer solutions. Competence-based trust instills confidence that the person you've sought out knows what she is talking about.

By using a network perspective to build key dimensions of relationships that yield effective collaboration, different interventions emerge that can promote a group's effectiveness. For example, team leaders can coach members on certain behaviors to improve the likelihood that they will be seen as trustworthy sources of knowledge. These behaviors include acting with discretion, showing consistency between word and deed, ensuring rich communication, engaging in collaborative dialogue, ensuring that decisions are fair and transparent, creating personal connections, giving first to promote reciprocity, and disclosing one's expertise and its boundaries.[46]

Question 6: Does Organizational Context Support Collaboration and Momentum?

Significant drains on productivity and employee morale will occur if a team-based design is inconsistent with an organization's strategy, information and performance management systems, leadership style, or employee skill base. The concept of *network momentum* is particularly helpful when considering team effectiveness and external forces that can dramatically shape collaboration. In any organization there are a variety of forces that support network development and those that degrade organizational networks. The balance of these forces will determine whether network momentum is positive or negative—and whether a team network, once strengthened and refined, will resist falling back into unproductive patterns.

Staff turnover is the single greatest factor that can degrade organizational networks. Other contributing factors, such as morale, overwork, internal competition, and poor leadership, can also hurt people's ability or willingness to connect with others in the support of organizational objectives. It stands to reason that what is needed to support network development is a strong organizational context composed of four critical elements: formal structure, work processes, development activities, and culture.

- *Formal structure.* Decentralized routine decision rights; latitude for work to be performed outside formal reporting lines and broker-liaison roles.
- *Work processes.* Diverse team structures designed to fill network gaps; flexible work flow and collaborative technologies.

- *Human resource practices.* Systematic exposure of capabilities across the organization; social and professional network opportunities and key external connection development.
- *Culture.* Values that support ad-hoc collaboration; recognition of external ideas and relationships and risk taking.

Conclusion

Our traditional notions of teams and teaming are being replaced by an understanding that performance and innovation are driven by an organizational capability to create productive collaborations rapidly among employees with relevant expertise, resources, and decision-making authority. Developing this capability is no small challenge in most organizations, where culture, leadership, and hierarchical reporting structures impede the flow of information, and excessive specialization disrupts collaboration. Leaders who manage these collaborations well are far more effective than those who simply form and disband teams in solving problems, delivering products, and capitalizing on client opportunities with the full range of resources and expertise in their organization.

In this chapter we have shown how a network perspective can improve team effectiveness through leveraging key relationships in networks. Specifically, leaders should consider three important steps:

1. Shift attention away from time-consuming team building efforts and onto initiatives that enable networks to integrate expertise, resources, and decision-making authority rapidly at the point of execution in organizations.

2. Focus network-building efforts on key teams in the organization. This chapter has demonstrated unique network dimensions commonly associated with performance in three

prevalent types of organizational teams: sales, innovation, and execution.

3. Define and help develop the critical relationships that must exist for networks to enable team success. These relationships will always be unique depending on the goals of a team and the strengths, contacts, and resources of its members. Nevertheless, Table 6.1 provides a guide to the six common network dimensions that leaders and their teams need to consider in building the most effective networks.

Part Three

ADAPTATION

How To Promote Flexibility Through Network-Centric Human Resource Practices

In much the same way that innovation is a vital process for rejuvenating products and services, talent management is a vital process for renewing an organization's creative energies and human capital. In this, the final part of the book, we encourage leaders to evaluate their own and their employees' network strategies and structures with an eye to how they can enhance (or retard) the personal ability to adapt. Networks themselves also need to adapt, to changing market conditions, demographic shifts, and the emergence of new technologies. In simple terms, you don't just design a network and walk away. Networks are dynamic, just as organizations and competitive environments are dynamic.

The next two chapters demonstrate the value of a network perspective for leaders as they address the challenges of adaptation. Leaders' ability to act as effective designers, integrators, and change agents depends heavily on their ability to connect with critical constituencies. To the extent that they are discon-nected, they reduce their ability to influence important behav-iors and, perhaps more important, to hear critical voices and garner corrective advice. Moreover, leaders need to find ways to replicate the behaviors that make high performance possible. As we'll show, high performers demonstrate not only consummate skills but also distinctive personal networks. And, finally, lead-ers must be concerned about the next generation of leaders and the generation after that. They need, whenever possible, to use their networks to scout for talent and, conversely, to encourage future leaders to make the most effective use of their own net-works so that they continue to grow and adapt to the world as it changes around them.

7

DRIVING PERFORMANCE BY REPLICATING HIGH PERFORMERS' NETWORKS

It was at the end of a daylong workshop we had run at one of the world's premier investment banks when the closing keynote speaker, former President Bill Clinton, began to talk about networks. Clearly the three hundred investment bankers in the room were tired—they had been together for twelve hours straight—but you could have heard a pin drop as Clinton described how networks had helped him throughout his life. His words gave a personal voice to the twenty years of research that has shown that people who make targeted investments in relationships outperform those who simply build ever-larger networks.[47] Personal networks can be as powerful as group networks for leaders interested in driving performance and innovation by improving individual connectivity throughout an employee base.

The investment bank where Clinton spoke had put in place a program to build connectivity among its top performers at the vice president and senior vice president levels. Although these employees often saw no immediate need to collaborate with those in different functions and offices, the bank's president knew that the benefits of cross-selling and delivering more holistic solutions to clients could be realized only by improving connectivity in networks of high performers that bridged functional and business unit silos.

These cross-function and business-unit collaborations were not occurring on a day-to-day basis. In fact, an ONA made clear that even within business units and functions—points in the organization where you would expect people doing similar kinds of work to be well connected—the high performers were not leveraging best practices, client leads, and the expertise of their peers. In one function—investment management—only 8 percent of possible ties existed; for the investment banking function, that figure was only slightly higher, at 12 percent. It was also very clear that there were few connections across functions. For example, there were clear breakdowns in collaboration between fixed-income and capital markets and between investment management and investment banking.

To address this problem, the leadership team brought the high performers together several times a year to promote networking within the organization, and they provided various virtual forums to help people connect across geographic barriers. These efforts were designed to promote cross-selling, but they also helped in the retention of top performers—especially those who had the biggest influence on the network—by lavishing a little extra attention on them and helping them to form even more productive personal networks. (See Figure 7.1 for the network of revenue-producing collaborations among this group.)

A large part of the day we spent with this group was devoted to helping each of the high performers think about building more productive personal networks. Of course, simply giving employees a hearty slap on the back and sending them off to make connections won't accomplish much. Too often, rising stars in organizations do well for a while but then fall into various networking traps. They may, as many self-help books advocate, build so many ties that they become overloaded; or they may unwittingly turn to certain kinds of people too much—for example, those who are at the same hierarchical level or in the same department,[48] those who are close in age or who come from similar backgrounds,[49] or those whose personalities just happen to be a good fit with their own.[50]

Figure 7.1. High Performer Collaborations With and Without Key Brokers

With key brokers

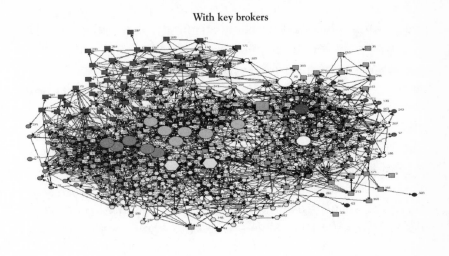

Without key brokers

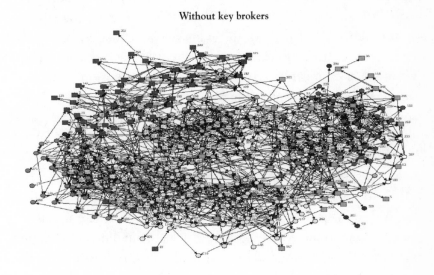

High performers, we have found, manage to avoid such traps. Instead of letting their networks become unwieldy and unbalanced, dominated by certain kinds of voices and lacking in others, high performers—for the same investment of time and effort required to maintain a large, happenstance network—intentionally build connections that boost their performance. We have developed a model of high performers' networks and networking behaviors that many organizations are using to drive effective network development into talent management processes such as hiring, on-boarding, career planning, and leadership development. These organizations employ this model as a starting point and then refine it to reflect the specific network characteristics that distinguish high performers in given roles.

At the investment bank, we conducted an ONA among a mixed audience of vice presidents (VPs) and newly promoted senior vice presidents (SVPs). Given the jump in compensation that occurs with this promotion, the newly minted SVPs were the envy of the room. When we described how these SVPs' networks were qualitatively different from the VPs' networks, we had everyone's attention. The message was simple but powerful for this audience: your network determines, in part, the size of your paycheck. But it is not just a big network that enables high performance. Instead, what distinguished the highest performers was a set of connections that bridged the organization in important ways and fought off insularity. For example, we were able to show that the SVPs' networks were more likely than the VPs' to connect to people in different business units, with different areas of expertise, and in different tenure groupings—people who had spent either less time or more time at the bank. And the ONA showed that the subset of people who had been promoted to SVP most quickly were the most effective in reaching out to people in these categories, as well as to people in different regions.

For the bank, building such networks at the individual level became a central objective—one that they hoped would both drive performance and improve retention rates among key players. When we revisited this group at year's end to see if those rates had in fact improved, we learned that retention rates were much better for this group than for the broader employee population. More important, though, was the fact that those who did leave had a far less substantial impact on the network than leaders had feared. After assessing the impact on revenue of those who had left the organization, we found that they had reduced revenue-producing collaborations by only 3 percent. This was less than one-sixth of the collaborations that could have been lost if the well-connected employees had been the ones who left, a result demonstrating that the talent program was effective not only in retaining high performers but also in minimizing the loss of value-added collaborations when departures did occur. Clearly this network focus on talent was an important one with substantial and quantifiable payoffs for the bank—payoffs that had remained invisible when the firm had considered its top talent as individual experts instead of also assessing their position in the larger network.

Replicating High Performers' Networks

Network analysis allows leaders to assess returns on talent-management programs designed to replicate the network drivers of high performers throughout an organization. Consider a network assessment of the large-gift fundraisers in one of the world's largest nonprofits. The fundraisers who brought in the most revenue weren't necessarily those who employed conventional fundraising strategies, such as targeting certain kinds of donors or engaging in various sales-management behaviors. Instead, high performers in this organization were distinguished by the kinds of interactions they had (both internal and external) and by the messages they delivered to donors. For example, they built external networks with both breadth and depth: 30 percent of their leads came from personal relationships (compared with 18 percent for the group as a whole), and they had more than twice as many cold-call leads as the group average. They also invested more time in building friendships with key donors—relationships that statistically were more likely to produce gifts in every range over $50,000.

What was most surprising was the central role the high performers played in the global nonprofit's internal networks. According to conventional wisdom, salespeople need to be well connected only externally; however, we found that if the organization lost the top 5 percent of its performers, income would fall by 23 percent and overall connections within the group would drop by 25 percent. Unfortunately, the people most affected would be the next tier of performers: On average, those ranked in the next 10 percent had significantly more and tighter relationships to the high performers than to others in the group.

Recognizing high-performer networks is only part of the story. Relevant network-building efforts need to be embedded in talent-management activities. In this nonprofit, leaders knew that those who stayed around longer developed better networks and produced more revenue, but they did nothing with this knowledge and lost a number of employees. To turn the situation around, the organization implemented programs—training that focused on replicating high performers' networks, revised account-planning practices that tracked network penetration in accounts, technology that helped leverage expertise within the organization, mentoring programs, and other efforts—to help low-tenure employees replicate the internal and external networks of high performers more rapidly. The anticipated improvements in retention rates were substantial, but factoring in revenue implications made this effort especially worthwhile. Simply helping newer employees replicate the networks of those with longer tenure increased revenue as much as 100 percent in certain development initiatives (and no less than 55 percent in the more transactional sales efforts).

Clearly, designing talent processes to identify and then build networks of high performers throughout an organization— whether through leadership programs, career management processes, staffing efforts, on-boarding processes, or mentoring relationships—yields a critical performance lever for leaders.

Research has long shown that fighting off insularity in one's network is associated with rapid promotion, better pay, job mobility, and higher performance evaluations.[51] Yet although such research has shown the benefits of bridging ties, less attention has been paid to the quality of relationships or behaviors that lead to effective networks.[52]

To expand our understanding of networks that enable individual performance, we initiated a research program to learn what makes for an effective personal network. We studied high performers—those in the top 20 percent of their organizations' human resources ratings—across a wide range of organizations in which meaningful performance data were available. This process yielded rich stories of success and identified common traps that high performers fall into when *not* attending to connectivity at key points in their careers.

We found that high performers' networks share three important dimensions:

1. *Structural:* High performers have a greater tendency to position themselves at key points in a network. They also fight off insularity and leverage the network around them more effectively to accomplish their work.

2. *Relational:* High performers tend to invest in relationships that extend their expertise and help them avoid learning biases and career traps.

3. *Behavioral:* High performers engage in behaviors that lead to high-quality relationships, not just to big networks.

People who do well on these dimensions—structural, relational, and behavioral—are more likely to be successful than those who pay little or no heed to their networks.

Next, in addition to further clarifying the network dimensions of high performers, we also discuss the network traps (summarized in Figure 7.2) that typically snare rising stars.

Figure 7.2. Common Network Traps That Derail Rising Stars

The bottleneck 	**Issue**: The bottleneck creates a heavy reliance on him- or herself. Bottlenecks use their own time—and that of others—inefficiently; they invisibly hold up work and innovation in the network. **Outcomes**: Bottlenecks may experience personal burnout; the organization's dependence on them means it fails to use expertise on the network's periphery, the network is often slow to respond to opportunities and threats, and innovation stalls. **Network remedy**: Identify categories of information, decision rights, and tasks that can be reallocated to alleviate overloaded points and draw others into the network.
The formalist 	**Issue**: The formalist has an inaccurate perception of the informal network and therefore fails to leverage it as a means to get work done. **Outcome**: Formalists may suffer personal frustration as things do not happen in the way they expect. In the organization, plans will be implemented ineffectively and opportunities will be missed. **Network remedy**: Identify brokers, marginalized voices, overloaded people and roles, and fragmentation where networks have fallen out of alignment.
The disconnected expert 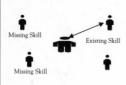	**Issue**: This otherwise high performer does not address skill gaps—deficiencies of technical expertise, decision-making ability, or interpersonal style—by leveraging relationships. **Outcome**: The disconnected expert will ultimately fail when a new role or changing times place demands on underdeveloped skills. **Network remedy**: Develop self-awareness and build ties to those who can help address skill gaps.
The biased networker 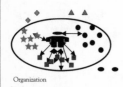	**Issue**: The biased networker allows certain voices (such as those with similar functional backgrounds, those in the same physical location, or those holding common values) to become disproportionately important in business decisions. **Outcome**: Poor strategies, inflexibility, and unethical decisions are all potential outcomes resulting from insularity or from allowing certain voices to become too privileged. **Network remedy**: Identify and correct overinvestment and underinvestment in relationships.

**Figure 7.2. Common Network Traps That Derail
Rising Stars (*Continued*)**

The surface networker	Issue: The surface networker engages in surface-level interactions to connect with others, but does not engage in behaviors that build a personal connection, sense of trust, and reciprocity critical to relationships that are truly helpful over time.
	Outcome: The surface networker's loose contacts tend to be effective only when he or she has something to offer, not when he or she is in need of help.

Network remedy: Use the network diagnostic to uncover self- and peer perceptions and modify behavior accordingly. |
| The chameleon | **Issue:** The chameleon absorbs the interests, values, and personalities of diverse subgroups, causing misalignment where alignment is needed. |
| | **Outcome:** Lack of alignment among key people and subgroups that need to work together slowly and invisibly drains momentum and effectiveness from the network.

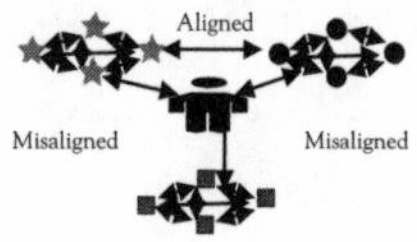

Network remedy: Use network techniques to discover where and how people need to be connected underneath the chameleon. |

The Structural Dimension: Bridging Positions in Networks

High performers tend to occupy network positions that bridge otherwise disconnected clusters of people. One way to visualize this phenomenon is by considering the game Six Degrees of Kevin Bacon, named for an actor who has appeared in a great variety of films in the course of his career.[53] Participants in the game attempt to name actors who are the most steps away from appearing with Bacon in a film. An actor who has actually appeared with Bacon is one step away, whereas an actor such as Michael Douglas is two steps away. Douglas has never appeared with Bacon himself but he did appear with Benjamin Bratt in the movie *Traffic*, and Bratt in turn appeared with Bacon in *The Woodsman*.

It turns out that it is difficult to name any actor from the history of film who is more than three steps away from Bacon.[54] But the magic in Bacon's network is not its size but how he is positioned within the movie universe. He is central—though not the most central, an honor that currently goes to Rod Steiger—because he has starred in a number of genres and so has ties spanning action films, comedies, thrillers, dramas, and horror movies. This stands in contrast to actors with similar numbers of movies under their belt but who have focused more narrowly on, say, comedies. Although those actors are highly connected within a genre, their lack of ties to other genres makes them much less central in the movie universe network.

All of this is not to say that Bacon is a great actor—you can be the judge of his cinematic success. Rather, it is to give a visual of how high performers manage their networks. In the workplace, people with networks like Bacon's do better than those with more closed networks, even when these colleagues maintain the same or a larger number of ties. People with insular networks tend to circulate with others who generally know about the same opportunities. For an equal investment of time, the Bacons of the world, with their more diverse networks, get a much greater return because they receive a wider variety of information early on and are able to capitalize on opportunities that require disparate expertise and insights.

Fighting off insularity in your network requires effort and runs contrary to the design of most organizations, whose formal structure, incentive schemes, physical layout, and even cultural values tend to encourage overly closed networks. Rather than fall into a comfortable trap of connecting with people who are themselves heavily interconnected, high performers tend to forge ties across important subgroups. As a result, they are better able to grab opportunities in the "white space" of a network than peers with more closed networks. Our research has confirmed that people who bridge subgroups are much more likely to be in the top 20 percent (as determined by performance reviews) of an organization.[55] Other research has shown that bridge builders tend to be promoted more rapidly, enjoy greater career mobility, and adapt to changing environments more successfully.[56]

For example, one well-known investment bank competed for and won the business of a major account from a rival bank, solely because the new banker (Dan) had collaborative ties to other product and service groups in his organization that the original banker (Geoff) lacked. Even though the client had been with the rival bank for years and had a strong personal relationship with the primary account executive (Geoff), Dan was able to leverage his network to deliver a more targeted and customized solution for the client.

In other words, despite the strength of the original relationship, the client was ultimately swayed by Dan's greater ability to produce results. When we interviewed the client, he explained, "It came down to a difference in delivery. Geoff should have been able to deliver the same service—I mean, they had all the same areas. But for some reason Geoff did not morph solutions to our changing needs in the same way Dan did." In the end, personal ties between Geoff and the client could not overcome Geoff's lack of connections to other parts of his own organization. "Part of it is that we are not set up for cross-selling," Geoff admitted. "My guess is that I could have done a better job connecting to groups that would have helped me think about a more complete solution. But that goes against the incentives here—at least in the short term—and so is something I need to go after myself."

How Rising Stars Go Wrong: The Bottleneck

Although they are extremely valuable to their organizations, bridge-building high performers such as Dan need to be aware of two network traps that can put an end to their effectiveness and career progression. In the first trap, the rising star, intent on forging ties with people in pockets across the organization, becomes a bottleneck because he or she is overloaded with requests. Some rising stars fall prey to their own need for control. They don't delegate tasks or decision rights or share information and thereby force others to rely on them. Although this strategy might make them an asset early on in their careers, these tendencies end up leading to excessive network demands that they can't meet as their responsibilities increase. As a result, they erode their own effectiveness and diminish the entire network's performance. Other rising stars become bottlenecks because they want to be experts, which means answering people's questions or solving their problems themselves rather than pointing people toward other resources or colleagues. Regardless of the root causes, bottlenecks end up using their time inefficiently, and they hold up work and innovation at myriad points in the network—a double penalty to the organization.

Consider Scott, a rising star within the professional services arm of one of the world's leading computer-manufacturing organizations. A network analysis of Scott's group revealed that more than fifty people turned to him regularly for information, and another fifty or so said they would be more effective if they could get more of his time. Scott was not a hoarder of information or decisions; indeed, he was well regarded and had vowed to minimize red tape and hierarchy. Even as his global group grew into the hundreds, he was adamant that it could be managed with only two layers of leadership and that he would remain accessible and open to everyone. But as his responsibilities multiplied, the approach that had made him successful early on became untenable. Scott pushed harder in the face of endless queries, opportunities, and challenges. He was working around the clock and it was entirely common for people to get e-mails from him at 3:00 or 4:00 in the morning. Ironically, his stand against red tape and hierarchy resulted in a gridlocked organization because the network had imploded on him and his small set of direct reports. Many people working in Scott's group became disgruntled when their queries went unanswered for weeks or, worse, disappeared into the ether.

The paradox of the bottleneck is that although these rising stars feel that everything is happening too rapidly as they race from meeting to meeting, where decisions are constantly being made, they actually slow down everyone around them. A fairly simple solution is to delegate, handing over categories of information and decisions as well as other tasks. Seemingly small decisions—such as travel approvals or pricing on routine transactions—can continually interrupt the rising star's more important tasks, but if he or she can't deal with them right away, others are kept waiting. Authority to make such decisions can often be reallocated through a policy document or made the domain of a less overloaded go-to person. This frees the rising star to pursue value-added work, reduces a hidden bottleneck, and draws other rising stars into the network.

Of course, delegating tasks is a well-worn managerial solution. A network perspective can make delegation more efficient and meaningful because it renders information and decision-making blockages visible. This matters on three fronts. First, being able to visualize relational demands for information or decision making tells rising stars where they need to either pare away ties entirely or simply decrease time spent with specific people. Second, a map of the network identifies those who should be go-to people—the people who have credibility in the eyes of their peers. Third, visualization allows leaders to model the potential impact of shifting relational demands in a network before they take time-consuming and potentially expensive action.

Interviewing a bottleneck to identify recurring informational requests and decisions that he or she can let go of is a simple and nonthreatening intervention because those duties are not central to the person's success. Unfortunately, if we return a year after following this process perfectly, we too often find high performers once again weighed down by minutiae and back in the bottleneck position. This behavior is partly a function of personality: despite the personal toll, high performers often like to be at the center of the action; they allow themselves to be drawn back in because it feels good to be needed and in the know. But others in the organization share responsibility for the situation: In order for a bottleneck to cast off responsibilities successfully, others must be willing to accept new duties, and they must be willing to choose courses of action on their own rather than continually seeking the overloaded person for advice.

How Rising Stars Go Wrong: The Formalist

Another way that rising stars go wrong is by relying too heavily on an organization's formal structure as a map of how work gets done. In doing so, these people fail to understand or leverage the power of informal networks. Although the lines and boxes on a formal organization chart should not be ignored—they do show an approximation of how power and resources are distributed—they can also mask or distort the underlying networks and collaborations that are the true currency of execution. Formalists miss important levers of influence when they fail to exploit these informal networks.

For example, Sidney Harman, founder of Harman Industries, a global manufacturer of high-fidelity audio and video products, recalls how excessive reliance on formal hierarchy and rules brought an important factory to a halt.[57] The problem resided in the polish-and-buff department of a plant located in Bolivar, Tennessee, where a crew of a dozen workers did the dull, hard work of polishing mirrors and other parts. On one fateful night, a malfunctioning buzzer failed to signal the start of a routine break period. Still, employees turned off their machines and headed for the coffee room. When shop management responded by ordering employees back to their machines for ten minutes, in Harman's words, "All hell broke loose."

What appeared to be a simple glitch brought to the surface a tidal wave of grievances stemming from management's rule-mindedness. As Harman later reported, it also illustrated how a handful of people in the informal network of the organization—senior machine operators, in particular—occupied vital-opinion leader positions and held the key to a much more effective way to run the factory. In fact, in the ensuing months and years, Harman revamped the factory and its workings, turning it into a kind of campus and encouraging a significant degree of worker control. Further, he created an environment where dissent was not only tolerated but encouraged.

Formalists miss the underlying network dynamics that can greatly improve the odds of success in implementing their plans. Research shows that managers vary in the accuracy with which they can describe the networks in their organization; those with more accurate perceptions are more successful over time.[58] High performers who continue to ascend throughout their careers identify intuitively the opinion leaders and work with and through them. They are able to address key fragmentation points in a network and do not let collaboration breakdowns undermine performance. They also recognize when formal and informal structure are becoming so misaligned that responsiveness and efficiency suffer because of work-arounds, poor role definitions, or process flows that do not capture how collaborative work is actually occurring in the organization.

So how can formalists be helped? By revealing to them what they have not been seeing, such as brokers, who can be tremendous change agents, or collaborative breakdowns deep within a network that are invisibly undermining performance potential. Assessing each network member's personal connectivity can also uncover employees who are more influential than it would seem on the surface and, conversely, those who have the ear of the boss but are much less effective in the eyes of their peers. Rising stars who avoid the formalist trap understand how to work through opinion leaders and shore up fragmented points in a network rather than let breakdowns in collaboration undermine performance. Formalists, in contrast, miss these seemingly invisible levers of influence and so are less effective over time.

The Relational Dimension: Managing Relationships That Extend Individual Expertise and Avoid Learning Biases

In addition to being positioned well within an overall network, high performers cultivate personal connections that extend their abilities and help them continually learn and develop. Technological progress over the past twenty-five years has not changed people's preference for relying heavily on others—whether colleagues or friends of colleagues—to find information and learn how to do their work.[59] Although it often makes sense to seek out human rather than technological assistance in solving business problems, there is a risk: people tend to gravitate to others who do what they do and see the world as they do. It's comforting, validating, and easy to interact with people who "get it"—who think as we do. Such tendencies, however, prevent otherwise high performers from extending their abilities, and decrease the odds of their developing truly innovative insights outside of their narrow domain of expertise.

This is not surprising; sociologists have extensively researched how people cluster in networks according to age, race, education, and gender. Unless forced to interact with others who are different, most people follow the strong tendency to seek out those who are demographically similar to themselves.[60] Interestingly, however, our research suggests that bridging these demographic social worlds is *not* what distinguishes networks of rising stars. Our high performers were no different from average or low performers in terms of the number or strength of ties to those with different demographic characteristics. Rather, they were distinguished by having people in their network who provided complementary (not similar) expertise and created bridges across aspects of formal structure.

Take the example of Steve, who in the mid-1990s became the director of innovation and technology in a global consultancy. His role was to learn what various operations were doing from a technology standpoint and to spread that knowledge throughout the firm. Through an enormous amount of travel, Steve quickly became a knowledge hub, identifying groundbreaking work in various offices of the firm around the world that others could leverage with their clients, and locating new practices and processes that could be adapted for use internally as well as with clients. Steve became highly successful in the organization and was promoted to the top executive ranks by 2000.

We came across Steve after a network analysis revealed him to have the broadest reach across functions, physical locations, and hierarchical levels that we had seen in all of our network analyses. His was not the largest network we had seen—in fact, it was not even the largest in that organization—but the number of ties bridging hierarchical levels, functional lines, and physical locations was stunning, and a factor to which Steve immediately attributed his success. Early in his career, those bridging ties were tremendously important in selling client work, developing a track record, and rising within the firm. As he ascended to the very top of the organization, those same relationships enabled him to implement global initiatives.

He remarked, "I think you see things differently when you have a better network. As you are listening to a client issue, you're not constrained. If I think of how I sell work or engage with clients, I am listening to their issues and immediately thinking about who I can loop in. You know, I could tell a client in New York that we just did that in Florida or Australia [and ask] 'Would you be interested?' This diverse network . . . rose with me as I have progressed in my career and has been the most important thing I have done in terms of my success. In an almost invisible way I know I am much more effective than people who are smarter than I am but haven't had the right experiences or motivation to build these relationships."

Consistent with Steve's story, our research shows three kinds of bridging ties to be important in high performers' networks:

Ties bridging hierarchical levels. A large proportion of high performers' ties span hierarchical levels. People higher in an organization can help a high performer make decisions, acquire resources, develop political insight, and gain awareness of opportunities in the organization. Those at the same level are generally most useful for brainstorming and providing specific help or information. And those at lower levels are often the best source of technical information and expertise.

Ties bridging functional and organizational lines. Rising stars are also much more likely than others to have ties outside their function (but inside the organization) as well as ties outside the organization. Further, they also have a strong tendency to make time to cultivate these relationships before they are needed. Then, when new opportunities come along, they are better able to visualize how they might integrate people into their network to provide a more comprehensive solution than their peers with less far-ranging networks could offer.

Ties bridging physical distance. The likelihood of collaborating with someone decreases substantially the farther one is from that person. Although collaborative tools such as e-mail, instant messaging, and videoconferencing can bridge some gaps, proximity still frequently dictates people's networks. Often this means that people allow proximate others—not those with the best expertise—to influence their thinking. However, our high performers were consistently much more likely to reach out across physical distance to connect with others who have relevant expertise.

How Rising Stars Go Wrong: The Disconnected Expert

Most high performers face transition points in their careers when they need to develop new skills to get to the next level. Unfortunately, skill gaps—whether related to technical knowledge, decision-making ability, or interpersonal influence—often manifest themselves when an emerging leader has little time to devote to learning. Those who keep moving and enjoying success find ways to augment individual abilities through their network.

Figure 7.3 paints a picture of the network of an up-and-coming manager in a major consumer products organization. Like many organizations, this one had a competency-based job categorization system. The Figure shows a subset of competencies and indicates that the manager turned to many people for help and advice on some competencies but only to one or two people on others. The initial conclusion might be that he needed more help with product quality, standards, and best practices, but in fact the opposite was true—those were the manager's strongest areas. Rather than leveraging relationships to augment his abilities, he was using his network to confirm what he already knew. The figure also reveals a second kind of bias. If Will and Keith dropped out of his network, he would have no one to turn to for help with vendor relations or consumer issues. Moreover, this reliance on two colleagues for advice in so many categories indicated a tendency he had to seek out trusted people for help with problems that lie outside their areas of expertise.

Figure 7.3. Extending Expertise Through Effective Networks

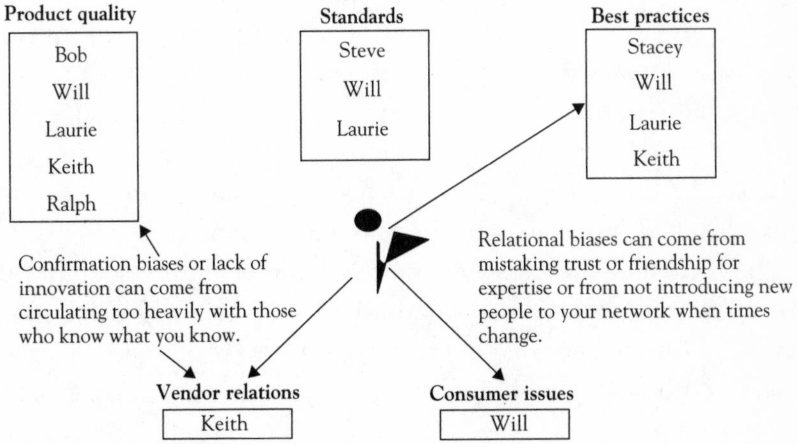

Product quality
- Bob
- Will
- Laurie
- Keith
- Ralph

Standards
- Steve
- Will
- Laurie

Best practices
- Stacey
- Will
- Laurie
- Keith

Confirmation biases or lack of innovation can come from circulating too heavily with those who know what you know.

Relational biases can come from mistaking trust or friendship for expertise or from not introducing new people to your network when times change.

Vendor relations
- Keith

Consumer issues
- Will

A network analysis like this one shows high performers two things they need to do to create a network that extends their abilities. First, they need to overlay their network on the skills demanded by a current or future role, which reveals where they need to initiate or deepen relationships to cover a weak spot. Second, they need to assess who they are going to for specific kinds of expertise to ensure that they are not ignoring those with relevant expertise in favor of familiar but less knowledgeable colleagues. It is common to rely on friends or trusted colleagues for advice, even in areas in which we may not have a great deal of expertise, because the conversations are comfortable. Yet personal effectiveness is of course undermined by continually mistaking trust, friendship, or simple accessibility for true expertise.

How Rising Stars Go Wrong: The Biased Learner

In this trap, the otherwise high performer allows certain voices—such as the voices of those who are physically nearby or who have a similar functional background or common values—to disproportionately influence learning and decision making. Take the case of Bob, a highly skilled individual hired to help turn around the R&D function of a major manufacturing organization. Because of his excellent track record, Bob had been hired away from a competitor to help boost quality and the pace of innovation in what had once been a highly regarded unit. This challenge was magnified because Bob did not know much about the inner workings of this two-hundred-person group spread across four countries.

Several months into his new role, Bob felt that he had made progress in integrating the efforts of the separate labs, but he wanted to test this belief with a network analysis. He was surprised to see that some steps he had taken to improve collaboration had actually resulted in a more hierarchical network, but he was perhaps most surprised when we began showing him different views of his own connectivity. Figure 7.4 shows a disguised summary of Bob's informational relationships with key scientists in the four countries. What is immediately obvious is that he was overinfluenced by those in his home location (Country 1) and heavily underinformed by those in Country 3 and Country 4. In fact, people in Country 4 would not even have been included in his network if it weren't for a single tie to someone he had known in a previous job.

On seeing the results of the analysis, Bob immediately recognized why he was having trouble implementing global programs and managing research efforts in Countries 3 and 4. He had become heavily attuned to the needs and concerns of those in

Figure 7.4. Visualizing Learning Biases

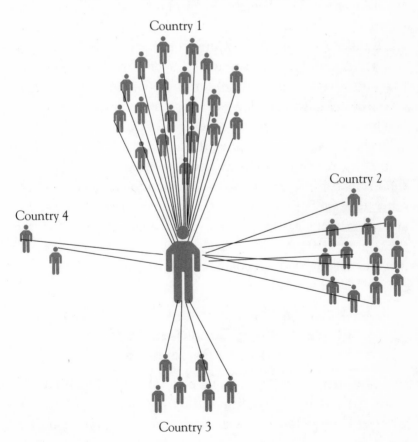

his home country, but was almost blind to the two remote locations and tended to view their concerns as gripes that he just
needed to push through. Such bias is extremely common and
can also crop up when rising stars are promoted but continue to
turn to those in the function or business unit they came from,
or when calendars are filled with the same colleagues over and
over, to the point that no new information or perspectives have
a chance to inform a rising star's thinking. Making these biases
visible is the first step in helping high performers increase or
decrease connectivity to ensure continued success.

Network biases afflict many organizations, particularly those
that are overtaken by hubris. Perhaps the most famous example
of an insular leader is Kenneth Lay, the late founder and CEO of
Enron. At that once-benighted firm, Lay gave the reins to "the
smartest guys in the room," Jeff Skilling and Andrew Fastow,
and he failed to heed the warning of someone from outside that
exclusive club, Sherron Watkins. Everyone knows the outcome.
In a somewhat less explosive example, Philip Purcell was recently
ousted from Morgan Stanley, partly for maintaining an inner circle
of advisers composed mainly of his former Dean Witter Discover
colleagues. People on the investment bank side who had been
with Morgan Stanley for years were frozen out. Purcell's firing of
three senior investment bankers prompted the resignation of two
other high-ranking executives, which enraged a group of dissident
alumni shareholders and set the stage for Purcell's removal from
the company.[61] This kind of excessive loyalty to members of one's
previous networks is both common and dangerous.

The Behavioral Dimension: Attitudes
and Networking Behaviors Associated
with High Performers

We consistently find that high performers distinguish themselves not just in the quality of their networks but also in the
beliefs and behaviors they exhibit in developing and maintaining their networks. Consistent with the theme of this book,

more important than the number of relationships they forge is the way their beliefs and behaviors create high-quality relationships. To be sure, our rising stars were active in reaching out to others, but they also invested well in relationships by giving first and by always being conscious of reciprocating favors or benefits received from others. (For greater detail on the specific behavioral dimensions, please see http://www.robcross.org.)

Consider Will, an executive who was hired into a major professional services firm to establish a critical practice. Although Will had built both domestic and international practices in other firms, he was unfamiliar with the culture and people in this new globally distributed organization and had little time to bring about substantial change. On top of that, he was given insufficient resources and people, so he had to establish credibility through high-quality client work while also tirelessly building his network with key partners.

One of the ways he built credibility was by joining a high-profile merger engagement that quickly resulted in additional sales. As stories of this and other successes spread, Will was increasingly drawn into engagements and sales opportunities, where he also established himself as a team player. Rather than looking for credit for each sale, he was happy to provide expertise and assistance as needed to ensure that others were successful. In addition, Will made it a personal goal to meet one hundred of the most senior partners within his first six months. Although this effort seemingly took time away from "real" work, these meetings not only generated future requests of Will's practice but also helped him to provide better support, because he knew each partner's background and goals.

Importantly, Will's efforts went beyond building reputation in the partner rank. He also focused heavily on developing and supporting those working with and for him. His willingness to jump in and help the team, regardless of the hour, became legendary among those lower in the hierarchy. In one instance, Will was on his way out the door at midnight after a long day at a client site. He could have just walked past a conference room where a team was working on a client deliverable, but instead he joined in and worked with them into the early hours of the morning, helping with the analysis and presentation. The return on such investments was greater commitment and effort from those in his practice. In addition, his reputation spread and created a pull in the internal labor market as other high performers jockeyed to work with him. These and other network investments rapidly increased Will's credibility and influence, and within only a year and a half he was asked to lead a much larger global practice within the firm.

How Rising Stars Go Wrong: The Surface Networker

The primary behavioral trap that rising stars fall into results from following conventional advice on how to be a good networker. Some high performers, as they emerge into leadership roles, know they have to be better at exerting influence through networks, but they choose to engage in superficial behaviors that do not build enduring relationships. A quick trip to Amazon.com reveals one of the problems: well over thirty books provide the secret of how to be a "power" networker or the like. What is the secret? Build a mammoth network of passing acquaintances. Although this advice is well intentioned, it turns out to be *completely different* from what high performers actually do. In fact, too often those who engage in such nonstop, superficial networking behaviors are the "politicians," "salespeople," or "office gossips" whom most of us duck into the nearest cubicle to avoid.

The surface networker's loose ties to a large number of people tend to be useful only when the networker can be a broker— that is, when he or she can create value by connecting others. Unfortunately, surface networkers often do not benefit from the reverse scenario: others bringing opportunities to them. And when things go wrong—which is often when you most need other people—surface networks do not help in the way that well-invested relationships with a history of trust, reciprocity, and maybe even true friendship do.

That was the experience of Susan, a product developer at a well-known consumer products organization. Her expertise and raw intelligence allowed her to succeed as an individual contributor on a wide array of technical projects. She got things done by brute force of intellect, attention to detail, and systematic follow-up. She always completed her projects successfully, which won her tougher assignments that eventually enabled her to develop a critical patent for a new process technology. In fact, Susan's performance and individual accomplishments were so strong that she became a favorite of senior technical leaders, who promoted her to a leadership role for a new product category initiative.

As she faced this transition, Susan was aware that working as a manager would require her to make new connections. She had learned through coaching and leadership programs about the necessity of working through others as she took on more responsibility, but she took only part of this advice to heart and focused little on developing trusted and reciprocal ties with peers throughout the organization. Although she built some relations up and down the hierarchy, most of her peers and direct reports were little more than names and faces to Susan. Her lack of strong lateral connectivity killed her when she tried to implement her efforts or needed the advice, expertise, or resources of colleagues in other departments. The situation was just as bad within her team. Over time, word got around: People worked behind the scenes to avoid being staffed on her project. Her new category project stalled, and she was eventually assigned to another category, with future advancement unlikely.

How Rising Stars Go Wrong: The Chameleon

The other behavioral network trap to avoid is being a chameleon. Chameleons are networkers who tailor their actions to fit whatever group they happen to be with at the time. High performers whose early influence was built on persuading those over whom they had no authority to do things for them are likely to fall into this trap. As these emerging leaders take on greater responsibility, their tendency to absorb the sometimes conflicting interests, values, and personalities of various groups makes them less able to achieve the necessary coordination and alignment among these groups. This tendency to blow with the prevailing wind is one of the few personality traits that has consistently been shown to have a negative impact on network patterns. It turns out that those who mold themselves to the values, interests, and dynamics of a given group fragment the overall network. By trying, for example, to appear as "one of the guys," a leader can inadvertently create impressions of favoritism, and the various subgroups in the network can lose sight of the overarching objectives that guide them all.

The consequences of the chameleon's changeability are particularly apparent when issues arise at the boundaries of legal or ethical behavior. Richard Nielsen, a specialist in organizational ethics, has noted that managers often find three important resources in short supply when they face ethical dilemmas: time, advice that can be trusted, and self-knowledge.[62] Time is critical because the pressure to act can short-circuit rational judgment; the absence of time, combined with the inability to get trustworthy advice and inadequate insight into one's own personal values and priorities, can be devastating. Managers make bad decisions when they don't know what they stand for, and a crisis is not the time to figure that out.

An example involving a corporate financial scandal illustrates the dilemma.[63] A senior financial executive for a commodities trading company was interviewed about making difficult decisions; the interview took place months before he was indicted by a federal grand jury for illegal accounting practices. When asked to whom he turned for advice when faced with ethical concerns, he answered, resolutely, "Myself." He prided himself on his self-reliance, and indeed his proclamation was a centerpiece in a rather adulatory article written about him in an industry magazine published the week after the interview. It turned out, however, that, like the proverbial lawyer who represents himself, his self-reliance proved foolhardy. Ultimately he folded under pressure from superiors to carry out illegal financial transactions. When he needed advice, he had no one to turn to and no time to conduct a search that might have revealed the thin ice on which he was being asked to skate.

Conclusion

It's easy to posit that appropriate, balanced connectivity contributes to the success of high performers, but traditionally it has been harder to describe in concrete terms how networks confer that advantage. As one senior leader told us, "We know high performers benefit from their networks, but we chalk up all the good things that happen to them to luck or good fortune. Like the travelers to Oz, we don't really have a good sense of what's going on behind the curtain." High performers often create their own luck by being more attuned to the network around them. Strategically leveraging relationships enables rising stars to see the big picture better, to generate innovative solutions by integrating the expertise of those with unique backgrounds, to position their efforts well, to bypass bureaucratic gridlock, and to obtain necessary resources and support.

In this chapter, we have shown how leaders can help to position rising stars at key points in networks, as well as how they can replicate high performer's networks rapidly and thoroughly throughout an organization. A series of steps are important for leaders to obtain the performance and innovation impact that are possible by leveraging individual employee networks:

1. *Shift from talent programs with an exclusive view of high performers as individual achievers to programs that also understand and help develop key network enablers of success.* This requires an understanding of how networks drive performance in a

given role. It also calls for development of talent and human resource programs that nurture key network dimensions as well as build individual skills and expertise.

2. *Pay attention to where and how high performers contribute to a network.* We typically find 30 to 35 percent of the high performers in a given role or organization to be extremely peripheral in the network. For some categories of employees this is okay. However, a large number of these high performers are not engaging in behaviors that allow the organization to get network leverage from their abilities.

3. *Ensure that recruiting, on-boarding, staffing, and development processes build productive rather than just big networks.* In this chapter we have shared three important network characteristics of high performers:

   Network structure: High performers build bridging ties and position themselves at key points in a network.

   Network composition: High performers invest in relationships that extend their expertise and help avoid learning and decision biases.

   Networking behaviors: High performers engage in behaviors that lead to high-quality relationships, not just big networks.

4. *Employ development and mentoring processes that help rising stars and leaders in career transition points avoid common network traps that derail careers.* These network traps will vary depending on social history, personality, hierarchical level, and to some degree role. Figure 7.2 provides a guide to the six traps that we have commonly seen undercut key employees.

8

SPEEDING PRODUCTIVITY IN NEWCOMERS AND AVOIDING KNOWLEDGE DRAIN

Whether they are growing to take advantage of a new market opportunity, restructuring to remain competitive, or simply trying to cope with attrition due to retirements and turnover, one thing is certain: organizations are increasingly dealing with newcomers. More than 25 percent of all workers in the United States have been with their company less than a year, and more than 33 percent, less than two years. American workers, on average, change jobs ten times between ages eighteen and thirty-seven.[64] As a result, speeding up the network development of new hires through more effective on-boarding has become a critical means of driving performance.

One of the many network challenges facing Anne Downing (the leader profiled in the Preface of this book) was the need to assimilate new people into her group rapidly. To manage the connectivity of the group as its membership increased, she implemented a system for both entry-level and experienced hires to quickly build personal networks that would help them succeed. The network analysis allowed her to plot connectivity against tenure and see who was integrating into the group well and who was not. Simple things like an e-mail of encouragement or an introduction between a struggling newcomer and one or more central people had an impact far beyond what she had anticipated. She laughingly indicated, "I remember the silence in the room when you started asking me about some of the peripheral people. Half of them I did not even know worked for me. So they had clearly fallen off my radar screen and in many cases would have been big losses."

In addition to paying great attention to several key players on the edge of the network, Anne also implemented processes to help connect newcomers in their first six to eight weeks. For example, upon arrival in her group, new hires were immediately given the names of ten people (all of whom had relevant industry or technical expertise *and* occupied central roles in the network) with whom to connect. These structured introductions gave the newcomer contacts and informed the central people in the network about the skills and experiences of the newcomer.

Anne also ensured that two other networks were formed for each newcomer. First, a buddy system was established that paired newcomers with peers at similar hierarchical levels and with roughly the same level of responsibility. Rather than try to reinvigorate a formal mentoring system that paired leaders with newcomers, Anne focused on peer mentoring and establishing relationships in which newcomers would feel comfortable asking sensitive or sometimes silly questions, like how to work the copier or what was politically acceptable in billing practices. She also established forums that helped newcomers "connect and commiserate" on a regular basis. A small fund was set aside for these people to get together at fun events, and teleconferences were held in which new hires from various sites could discuss common project issues.

Finally, Anne launched a shadowing program that put new hires on a client project for three weeks at no cost to the client other than travel and hotel expenses. This practice flew in the face of the firm's conventional wisdom, according to which people worked on internal projects until a paying client came along. But an assessment of Anne's practice one year later showed a remarkable impact from these relatively simple efforts. This follow-up network analysis clearly showed that newcomers were becoming embedded more quickly and that business results were being generated from this improved connectivity. The ratio of managers to analysts was declining rapidly, which meant that new, more junior people were being brought on board, integrated into the network, and made productive more quickly than had been the case before these simple shifts were made. As one newcomer put it, "The effort everyone makes to help integrate you really shows. You know people care and it makes all the difference."

Driving Productivity Through Effective Network Development in On-Boarding

The first and most obvious challenge with newcomers is to jump-start their productivity. New hires are often a net drain on an organization—drawing a salary, incurring training and orientation expenses, and consuming coworkers' time without providing much in return. A study by Mellon Financial Corporation found that productivity lost due to the learning curve for new hires and transfers is between 1 and 2.5 percent of total revenues. On average, the time for new hires to achieve an acceptable level of productivity ranges from eight weeks for clerical jobs to twenty weeks for professionals to more than twenty-six weeks for executives.[65] In today's fast-paced, competitive economy, organizations obviously cannot afford this kind of productivity lag.

A second challenge lies with realizing the creativity of new hires. Newcomers are potential sources of fresh ideas, perspectives, expertise, and industry contacts. However, many leaders find it difficult to leverage the creative energies of their new employees, and most newcomers are quick to express frustration in getting their ideas heard. In successful organizations with strong cultures, newcomers are not heard until they have gained visibility and legitimacy in the eyes of their peers. One experienced hire we encountered—a very senior consulting partner—noted that to be taken seriously, senior-level, experienced hires "have to become insiders in the firm, and of course this takes two or three years, during which most of us laugh about forgetting the unique insights we originally had, or we have just gotten tired of trying to push good ideas uphill."

The third challenge is keeping creative, productive new-comers in the organization long enough to justify the costs of recruiting, hiring, and bringing them up to speed. The probability that a new employee will quit reaches a peak after one and a half years and declines rapidly after that, so clearly, helping new-comers past this awkward entry stage is critical.[66] Yet ask most any executive about his or her success in retaining experienced hires and you are likely to see a pained expression. Although great sums of money and time are spent bringing these people into the firm, strong cultures or established networks often marginalize their contributions and keep them feeling like outsiders. When a highly skilled newcomer leaves, the organization not only loses its investment in that individual but also suffers from a loss of momentum as remaining employees struggle to compensate for the newcomer's absence and readjust to his or her replacement.

In general, when organizations do anything at all to orient new hires, most take what we call an informational approach—overloading newcomers with information about company routines and technologies and expecting them to have the background, skills, and cognitive ability to filter, comprehend, and internalize the information.[67] In some cases, however, we have found model organizations that use a relational approach to foster well-connected networks for newcomers. Rather than providing an overwhelming amount of information, these organizations help newcomers establish a broad network of relationships and then let them tap their growing information network to become productive contributors quickly. This approach doesn't have to be time consuming or expensive, but it does require managers to avoid the following five common practices and assumptions that slow the integration of new employees. These subtle shifts in thinking can reveal simple, but often overlooked means of helping newcomers become connected and productive.

Don't assume that your best newcomers will effectively onboard themselves. Implicit in many organizations is the assumption that onboarding is up to the new hire; the organization just needs to hire the right people and they will get themselves up to speed quickly, learning what they need to know on their own and asking others for help and advice when they get stuck. This expectation is especially true for experienced hires. As one investment banker reflected, "Leadership thinks we are paying our experienced hires an ungodly amount of money and that they damn well better be able to hit the ground running and get connected themselves." Although these organizations may provide training and orientation, they often assume that newcomers are responsible for their own assimilation and are quick to blame failures on either a lack of effort by the newcomer or poor fit with the organization.

The problem is that many of the qualities that organizations want in new hires—intelligence, experience, and independence—tend to reduce the new hires' willingness to ask for help from colleagues or to engage in exploratory conversations with key resources. These people often feel tremendous pressure to prove themselves—and fast. They fear that asking questions might reveal their ignorance and that engaging in open-ended brainstorming conversations with colleagues might distract them from producing results. Top organizations are increasingly providing new employees with a window of opportunity in which they can, penalty free, be exactly what they are: newcomers who can legitimately seek help and advice from coworkers and engage in exploratory conversations in order to understand the skills, abilities, and knowledge of other employees.

Bank of America judges the first twelve months to be a critical time for new executives and puts considerable effort into helping them understand the business and the organization's culture and leadership style. It does so by immersing new hires in a network from the time of their final interview. Key relationships—with bosses, peers, other new hires, and people performing similar work in different locations—create a set of concentric circles for each new hire. Onboarding processes and manager training can help avoid either the lack of network development or insular connectivity by finding ways to encourage newcomers to ask questions, by telling others to expect and respond to questions from newcomers, and by reassuring new hires that the only "stupid questions" are the ones not asked.

Don't just give newcomers a lot of information to help them get up to speed quickly. Unfortunately, most organizations consider onboarding to be primarily a process of information transfer in which the key to rapid productivity is to provide newcomers with plenty of information about the company, their initial project, and the resources they need to complete it. Some of this information is indeed critical. In our interviews, however, newcomers never mentioned the typical onboarding program as the key to getting up to speed quickly, and when we've compared the experiences of rapid onboarders with those of slow onboarders, documentation and training have never been the differentiating factors.[68]

The best onboarding practices mix information delivery with network development. When we've asked newcomers what they found useful about their initial training and orientation, the most frequent response has been not the content they receive but the chance to meet other newcomers and coworkers. When newcomers approach with questions, leaders should fight the tendency simply to provide the requested information and look instead for opportunities to connect them with experts and key resources. For example, Whirlpool Corporation's Young Professionals' Network serves as an important vehicle both for enhancing business performance overall and for onboarding new employees.[69] New hires are encouraged to find an area of interest—business impact, talent development, or community—as part of their early orientation to the company. Such an interest accelerates integration into existing networks and addresses valued goals.

The most successful programs have more than cocktail hours and instead provide structured activities to push newcomers both to meet and to engage with a diverse set of other new hires as well as with established employees who themselves are well placed in the organization's network, rather than just clustering with those they get to know early on. At the same time, leaders should ensure that organized training and orientation programs are not excessively lecture based and include time for socializing. And they should also fight the temptation to put all initial training online. Relegating such an important process to cyberspace has a dramatic impact on networks over time.

Don't rely on introductions to happen serendipitously during onboarding. Leaders often assume that introductions occur naturally as newcomers encounter team members in project meetings or meet coworkers in hallways. Unfortunately, the reality is that people are typically too busy to help care for a new coworker without some specific guidance. In comparing the experiences of rapid onboarders and slow onboarders, one of the most consistent differences we found is the use of planned, strategic introductions between newcomers and key resources.

Besides taking the time to introduce newcomers personally to certain established employees, managers can also use meetings, lunches, and company gatherings as opportunities to get newcomers face-to-face with a variety of coworkers. Some companies use their computer-based expertise locators to help new hires learn something about their coworkers (and vice versa), knowing that having information beforehand helps reduce the awkwardness of first meetings. One company puts baseball-card-like posters of newcomers on office walls to introduce them to coworkers and help facilitate introductions. A startup in Silicon Valley puts helium balloons in the newcomer's cubicle on the first day and expects coworkers to introduce themselves. The HR manager commented that "they are a good way to welcome somebody, are very festive, and the new hire can find her cube more easily. Plus it lets others know that a new person has arrived." Starbucks has its own internal virtual community, a MySpace look-alike that clarifies the skills needed for each job; more than sixty thousand employees use it to test-drive new jobs, inquire about work styles in different parts of the world, and pursue career interests.

Don't assume that a good first assignment is small, compact, and quickly achievable. One of the biggest, most consistent differences between fast and slow onboarders is the degree to which their first assignment requires them to build relationships with a wide variety of people. Newcomers with stand-alone projects often remain isolated and don't build the relationships they need to be really productive in the long term. Lacking a network of relationships, they often feel less connected to the organization, less satisfied with their progress in "fitting in," and more likely to leave. That's why at retailer Best Buy new female managers are encouraged to join the Women's Leadership Forum (WOLF).[70] Through WOLF they have the opportunity to tackle important but complex problems—such as how to grow the company's share of the female market—in addition to their new jobs. Each WOLF team chooses a project and then has to get ideas into a few stores in three months and into many stores in six months. According to Best Buy, turnover in female managers has dropped 10 percent since the inception of the program.

In the words of one executive, a good first assignment helps the newcomer become "spider-webbed into all parts of the organization." Managers need to create strategies to facilitate good initial relationship development. They might design the newcomer's first project so that it cannot be completed without assistance from coworkers. They can also assign newcomers to cross-functional project teams that expose them to a broad network of resources or, alternatively, give them the opportunity to develop unique expertise so that other members need to talk to them to complete their own work.

Don't rely on a mentoring program as the sole solution to integrating new hires. Research has shown that newcomers in supportive mentor relationships are more satisfied and committed to the organization; as a result, many organizations emphasize mentoring soon after entry.[71] What often separates rapid onboarders from slow onboarders, however, is not the presence of a formal mentor but the presence of a buddy, someone the newcomer can comfortably ask trivial questions (How does the e-mail system work? How do I order supplies?) or political questions (Whose opinion really matters here?). Like a mentor, a buddy can be someone officially assigned by a manager, or simply a nearby coworker who naturally emerges as an accessible resource and confidant.

Why are buddies more important than mentors? Right after they join the organization, newcomers are more concerned with deciphering norms and routines than they are with developing their careers. They are often reluctant to ask senior managers (who might formally be their mentors) questions that might reveal the newcomer's ignorance of concepts they should have known before they took the job. Through buddies, newcomers can quickly get basic questions answered, test emerging ideas about organizational norms and taboos (Do people really dress up for client meetings around here?), and quickly get referrals for more specific questions (Who knows the most about the technology behind the Phoenix Project?).

Buddies also help newcomers establish information relationships with coworkers in ways that can't easily be facilitated by their managers. A positive initial experience with a receptive and supportive buddy can also reduce a newcomer's reluctance to ask questions of other coworkers. Although mentor relationships are extremely valuable, they don't typically provide the access to basic company information that newcomers need to become confident, productive members quickly.

Avoiding Costly (But Often Invisible) Knowledge Loss in Networks

On the other end of the human resources value chain are departures and transitions, and the knowledge loss that results when well-connected employees leave or move into new roles. This is a phenomenon that both public and private sector organizations are increasingly struggling with. Aging baby boomers present a major challenge to organizations: more than 20 percent of the American workforce holding executive, administrative, and managerial positions is set to retire by 2010. Critical knowledge loss also occurs, however, as a result of job mobility and alternative work arrangements, as well as when established employees quit or contract workers (representing one in six American workers) move on to other organizations.[72]

No matter how employees leave, the reality is that most organizations do not guard against this very real and costly resource drain. Employees depart with more than *what* they know—they leave with critical knowledge about *who* they know. Lose these networks, and a substantial impediment to getting work done and responding to new opportunities arises.

ONA gives leaders two views that help them manage and guard against knowledge loss. First, network analysis lets leaders identify key knowledge vulnerabilities in a network by virtue of both what a person knows and how his or her departure will affect a network. Second, it gives leaders the ability to address knowledge loss unique to three network roles—central connectors, peripheral players, and brokers—each of which holds specific categories of knowledge.

Of course, beyond being concerned with information flows, leaders are also often interested in assessing value creation and economic return from key personnel, relationships, or entire networks. As we discussed in Chapter 4, this relational view of effectiveness quantifies the value lost by the departures of those who may not be high on the formal organization chart but are instrumental to the inner workings of an organization. For example, relationships in the network diagram in Figure 8.1 reflect estimates of time saved as a result of interactions among members of a community of practice in a financial services organization. Each member estimated the typical amount of time saved per month as a result of resources, information, and help received

Figure 8.1. Putting a Value to Key Departures

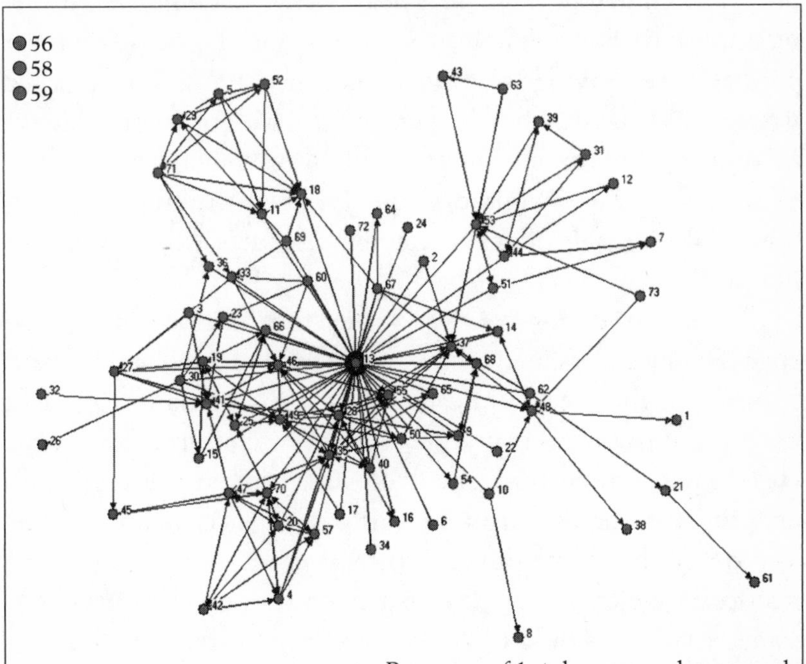

Response of 1 + hours saved per month

Savings for the past month: **1,035 hours** Converted to $ at $100/hr **$103,500**	**Potential time and $ saved per month** Person 13: 213 hours ($21,300) Person 53: 66 hours ($6,600) Person 49: 46 hours ($4,600) Person 41: 40 hours ($4,000) Person 70: 37 hours ($3,700)

from other members of the community. Although we can measure value creation relationally in other ways (such as revenue creation and economic value added), here our approach allowed us to quantify the value of this network by multiplying time savings by a fully loaded compensation figure for each worker.

It turned out that twenty members of this community added no value at all (in terms of time saved), although many were fairly seasoned employees who could and should have been helpful. More important, the analysis revealed a handful of people contributing a great deal of time-saving value to the organization. For example, the most central person, number 13, generated savings of $21,300 per month. When we asked what would happen if that person left, we got a long silence in response. It turned out that she was in fact leaving. The managers of this organization quickly used the network analysis results to help identify emerging leaders who could take her place.

Through the lens of ONA, leaders can also see the knowledge held by central connectors, peripheral players, and brokers. It turns out that people in each of these roles tend to be sought out for unique kinds of information, and retaining this knowledge requires more than simply documenting employees' skills and expertise areas. Organizations can replace an individual's knowledge, but more difficult to recover are the network connections that enable work to get done in a given context. As summarized in Table 8.1, a close look at the three network roles and the specific knowledge associated with each role can help organizations identify critical network-related knowledge to retain and the potential means to do so.

Central Connectors

Central connectors are the people who have many direct information-seeking relationships. Typically they have a high level of expertise in one if not many areas (although occasionally people are in this role owing to factors such as job design or political posturing). Because of the help they give to others, they also have a strong awareness of expertise in the network and are likely to receive assistance if they ask for it because of the social capital they have accumulated. They make day-to-day work possible for many others and are critical when things go awry; as such they are often the first called on in crisis situations.

Table 8.1. Unique Knowledge Retention Strategies by Network Role

Network Role	Knowledge Loss Risks	Actions
Central connectors (have many direct information-seeking connections, defined by degree)	Loss of technical expertise and organizational memory as well as a set of relationships that help many colleagues get information or other resources to do their work	Use personal network profiles in career development and onboarding practices to create network redundancies where departures might dramatically fragment a network.
		Reallocate information access and decision rights to ensure that key points in the network do not become too vulnerable.
	Loss of experiential knowledge and reputation that enable rapid onboarding	Have central connectors lead communities of practice as a means of creating connections around them.
		Require central connectors to help onboard newcomers through strategic introductions, shadowing, mentoring, and joint projects.
Brokers (have many bridging connections, defined by betweenness)	Loss of broad knowledge of how the organization operates and the ability to recognize opportunities requiring integration of disparate expertise	Identify and develop brokers through staffing and rotation across division, geography, and expertise groups.
		Assign brokers strategically, where information gaps exist or where ideas can move from concept to action.
	Loss of the ability to mobilize and coordinate efforts of disparate groups in the pursuit of opportunities	Give brokers preauthorized decision limits to tap into network resources. Allow them to experiment to obtain real-time information.
Peripheral players (have few direct information-seeking connections, defined by degree)	Loss of niche expertise or early adopter ideas that have the potential to reshape offerings or operations	Pair peripheral people with brokers or central connectors or both to bootstrap them into the network.
		Ensure that relevant peripheral people are visible and engaged; encourage project mobility, speak at "lunch-and-learns," and give Webcasts.
	Loss of external relationships built on trust and familiarity	Invite external partners to conduct workshops and attend meetings in order to broaden their network.
		Reward employees for bringing external ideas and connections into the organization.

Some answers they provide themselves, but many they acquire through other people, who help them think about key challenges or obtain technical information.

Losing a central connector can mean losing deep, network-embedded technical expertise that is critical in both day-to-day operations and times of crisis. Employees seek out central connectors for various reasons, but one of the most prevalent and important motivations is to obtain deep subject-matter expertise. Often the knowledge that central employees possess is what Dorothy Leonard and Walter Swap refer to as "deep smarts": expertise based on experiences, intuitive judgments, and the ability to analyze problems from multiple perspectives.[73]

To reduce the network burden on central connectors and decrease the impact of key departures, organizations need to develop the collaborative skills of everyone in the network and then help position emerging connectors in the center of the network by assigning them to critical and relevant projects. Leaders should embed personal network assessments into career development and onboarding processes for new hires by using a work project in which people learn when and how to rely on others.

Organizations also need to create structured ways to retain the organizational memory held by central connectors. Selecting centrally connected network members for informal knowledge transfer rather than simply using those employees in formal roles always yields more consistent results. A pharmaceutical company, for example, that needed scientists to work together to interpret a voluminous amount of data paired junior scientists with centrally connected ones. The central scientists provided real-time feedback and helped build the junior scientists' relationships throughout the organization. We found a similar arrangement in a consulting firm where junior consultants shadowed partners by attending meetings with them, listening to day-to-day discussions, and watching them perform their work.

These kinds of programs are effective even for experienced hires. Although newcomers might have a lot of great ideas, they rarely have insight into the norms, politics, or work practices of their new organization. Central connectors are the best possible advisers in this regard.

Brokers

Brokers have ties across subgroups and therefore have a disproportionate ability to help an organization capitalize on opportunities requiring the integration of disparate expertise. They may not have the most connections in a network, but by virtue of their relationships across subgroups, they have a unique understanding of the political dynamics and of the resources and expertise embedded in a network. When they leave, they often impair an organization's ability to spot opportunities that require the integration of expertise and resources to coordinate efforts among people with different perspectives and values.

The departure of brokers does not affect as many people as the departure of central connectors, but it can disproportionately fragment an overall network at key junctures. We can see this effect in the network diagrams of the innovation function in a professional services organization (Figures 8.2 and 8.3). Mary, employee 29, has connections in research and in the business units, as well as with her colleagues in business development. If we remove the top five brokers—employees 53, 56, 54, and 47, as well as Mary—we see significant disruption to the network. Two of the research clusters become nearly isolated, and the connections between the research side of the organization and the business unit and development groups become sparse. One manager who saw this diagram was surprised that some of these employees were brokers, because they weren't as central or as visible as some of the other employees.

Figure 8.2. Information Network of a Services Organization by Group

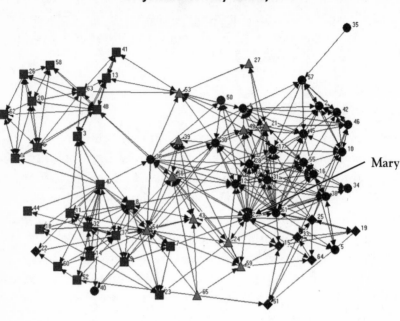

Mary

Group

| ■ Research | ▲ Business units | ● Business development | ◆ Other |

As organizations struggle with silos driven by formal structure, deep technical expertise, or occupational subcultures, brokers become increasingly important. Unfortunately, however,
the type of relational knowledge and organizational perspective
they hold is rarely reflected in retention programs. The irony
is that when brokers leave, many organizations don't even know
what has been lost.

Three practices can help leaders identify, develop, and position brokers in their networks:

1. Leaders can encourage and reward lateral movement across
   projects, divisions, and geographies through job rotation.
   Brokers possess unique knowledge that allows them to integrate disparate groups, but this knowledge is gained only

Figure 8.3. Information Network of a Services Organization with Top Five Brokers Removed

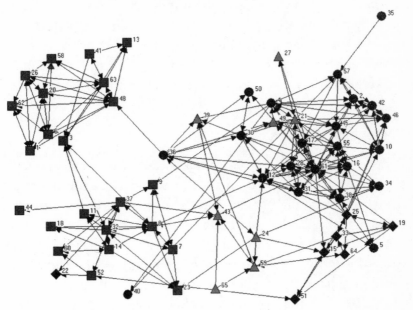

through experiences that provide a deep understanding of expertise, subcultures, and work processes.

2. Leaders should identify and groom potential brokers by performing an ONA to see who currently plays the role or who fits the profile. A potential broker will be well-tenured and have high credibility, will have worked in different groups, and will be an effective translator and negotiator. Once identified, a broker can be trained to integrate networks by establishing contacts in multiple groups, understanding the needs and objectives of each group, and looking for win-win opportunities through the transfer and application of ideas.

3. Leaders need to assign or position brokers thoughtfully in business processes and strategic initiatives. Brokers belong where tighter integration between groups would be a benefit

to the organization or where new ideas can move from the concept stage to actionable results, such as between research and development groups and business units. And of course fully implementing brokers may mean giving them greater authority or more flexibility in decision rights. It's not enough for them to see opportunities and threats in the marketplace; they must also be able to act on them.

Peripheral Players

Peripheral employees are so called because they have the fewest ties. From their position on the boundary of the network, many peripheral players feel that their knowledge and expertise are marginalized. They are not as visible within the company as central employees or brokers are, and as a result they are usually ignored when it comes to knowledge retention strategies. This can be a mistake. Although these people may be peripheral in the network of the organization they work for, they often are very well connected externally.

Peripheral people we interviewed typically had niche expertise. In daily operations, the loss of this expertise would not be a big deal—but when crises arise, it could bring things to a dramatic halt. Peripheral people also tend to have novel insights and can be substantial sources of innovation because they often are not steeped in existing paradigms and can combine fresh insights with an understanding of the inner workings of an organization to generate feasible innovations.

It is important to include peripheral employees in any knowledge-retention strategy. One effective practice is to connect them to brokers. In our work with companies, we can usually identify the top ten or so brokers or "influencers" in the network. Then, by connecting each broker to someone peripheral in the division, for example, the overall connectivity of the network rises dramatically. In one one-hundred-person network we were able to achieve a 25 percent increase in cohesion (the average distance information travels to cross the entire network) by establishing connections from the top twelve brokers to people in their division who resided on the periphery.

It is also wise to get peripheral members involved in activities that make them feel connected to the organization and that alert others to their expertise. This involvement may include encouraging mobility across projects so that the peripheral person can experiment and bring in new ideas. Peripheral workers can also be made visible by giving them the opportunity to do Webcasts or teleconferences and lunch-and-learns on the work they are doing, or they can be encouraged to join a community of practice. These activities give them the opportunity to meet people who have similar interests and keep them engaged.

In addition, although peripheral people may not be well connected within their own organizations, it is a mistake to assume they are not part of an extensive external network. These outside relationships represent a much less obvious but nontrivial risk of knowledge loss. Our research has shown that peripheral employees, on average, have roughly as many relationships outside the organization as central employees have within the organization. We see common examples of this in sales divisions and research groups. If the departing employees take their contacts with them as they walk out the door, the loss to the organization could be deep insights about markets, technologies, and products; understanding of customer requirements; and relational capital critical to sales efforts.

Companies can more systematically maintain these hidden external relationships developed by peripheral people by inviting the outsiders to conduct workshops, give presentations, or sit in on meetings to provide feedback. Connections can then develop between more employees and the external partner. You may even want to reward individuals for bringing external contacts and their expertise into the organization. In many organizations there's a disincentive for employees to share their contacts, so a change in the reward system may be needed.

By recognizing and rewarding joint sales efforts, an organization encourages the sharing of external relationships instead of reinforcing a go-it-alone mentality to maximize personal monetary commission and recognition. In one example, a pharmaceutical company rewarded scientists who published papers with both an external partner and another colleague.

Conclusion

Simple shifts to onboarding approaches can have a dramatic impact on productivity and innovation. Leaders can capture greater productivity from their new hires by facilitating introductions between the newcomers and key resources as well as by ensuring that new employees quickly build a network of trusted relationships. Instead of asking only *What do our newcomers need to know?* organizations must also ask, *Whom do our newcomers need to know?* On the other end of the human resources value chain, leaders can help stem knowledge loss from key departures when they view such departures not just as specific expertise walking out the door, but also in terms of how a departure affects a network's ability to function. A close look at the three network roles, and the specific knowledge associated with each role, can help organizations identify critical knowledge to retain and the potential means to do so.

In this chapter we have shown how more advanced organizations take action to both speed up onboarding of key employees and minimize the relational impact of departures. Toward this end, leaders can take specific steps to

- Shift onboarding processes so that rather than simply providing an overwhelming amount of information, the organization helps newcomers establish a broad network of relationships that they can tap in order to become productive contributors quickly. This approach doesn't have to be time-consuming or expensive, but it does require managers to avoid the five common practices and assumptions described in this chapter that slow the integration of new employees.

- Minimize knowledge loss when key people leave by employing career development and staffing practices that fill network holes created by potential departures before such people leave. A network approach allows organizations to identify the specific knowledge loss occurring with the departure of people in certain network positions (as outlined in Table 8.1) and to prepare accordingly to minimize network disruptions.

9

THE ROAD AHEAD: EMERGING OPPORTUNITIES FOR THE NETWORK PERSPECTIVE

A network perspective helps leaders in three of their most critical tasks: aligning people around strategic objectives, executing essential processes, and adapting to change. By rendering visible what is often invisible, network analysis makes it possible for leaders to better understand and manage the resources—people, ideas, relationships—at their disposal and to increase the accuracy with which they can intervene to improve innovation, resource allocation, and talent management. The same concepts and tools help leaders judge how much alignment and collaboration they actually need, and what impact they can achieve through focused investment. Indeed, much of the power of a network perspective derives from its ability to help leaders make the right connections—not from everyone to everyone else, but from the right people to others in the right ways to achieve specific goals.

The case studies and examples we've provided demonstrate that the network perspective has advanced from theory to practice. Businesses, government agencies, and not-for-profits alike are dramatically improving performance by diagnosing—and where appropriate, redesigning—the human relationships through which knowledge flows, the processes through which critical objectives are achieved, and the paths of communication essential to alignment. It is an overstatement to suggest that the network perspective represents a new management paradigm; after all, many of the core ideas have been around for decades. What is new, however, is the progress that has been made in rendering those ideas actionable.

Practical application and experimentation are also revealing new insights and opportunities for further refinement of the perspective. The four dimensions of networks that we believe have tremendous potential are visualization, emotion, design, and cognition.

Visualization: Seeing Organizations

Not far into the future, we will see as well as manage organizations very differently. Whereas today we rely on two-dimensional, static, and notoriously outdated organization charts to depict what an organization is or does, soon we will be able to represent companies, even industries, the way they really are: active, in motion, growing, shrinking, flowing in the direction of opportunities, pulsating with life, and inevitably fading out of existence. The new organization chart is likely to be a network movie, a dynamic visual representation that will provide powerful new insights into how an organization is working, and critical warning signals about the places and the ways in which it isn't.

The implications of visualization for leaders are profound. Suppose investors and leaders of a rapidly growing company want to know whether their acquisitions are being integrated into the culture and operations of the existing firm. Are key people talking to one another? Do newcomers feel like they belong? Will the benefits they bring be eroded or amplified? Questions like these can be partially answered today through conventional surveys and interviews, but the results are usually skewed by who does the interviews. Further, when such tools are administered alone (that is, without the insights that come from relating survey responses to informal networks of communication and influence or trust), the results can be hard to interpret. Yearly climate or employee satisfaction surveys are often insufficient; by the time a critical issue surfaces, it may be too late to address it.

Suppose, by contrast, that an animated rendering based on multiple unobtrusive sources of information revealed that key people in some of the acquired units were drifting toward the margins of the organization, exchanging e-mails only with each other and appearing for all the world to be on their way out. Suppose the same view showed that newcomers who worked for company veterans of similar functional background or demographics were much more involved in exchanges with peers and counterparts and obviously integrated into the daily life of the enterprise. The cues provided by a dynamic visualization—quite literally, a movie of who is collaborating with whom—would most likely focus energy on getting the marginalized people better connected before they left altogether. Would the movie replace the survey or the site visit? Unlikely, but at a minimum it would dramatically enhance the quality and timeliness of information for nervous leaders and investors.

As illuminating as network diagrams can be, they are still in an early stage. Although they enable us to see beneath the surface better than ever before, we still cannot see the froth and motion that characterize a living organization. Fortunately, our ability to portray organizations as things-in-motion is catching up with the theory. Software now enables us to track in real time the exchanges and interactions (such as orders and payments, phone calls and e-mails, arrivals and departures of products and people) that are an organization's circulatory system.[74] New algorithms can detect patterns of communication and information exchange. A relatively inexpensive microprocessor can animate or string together network "snapshots" into a motion picture, which can in turn be accelerated to show that organizations and even industries evolve in much the same way as time-lapse photography has made it possible for us to see a seed germinate and flower in a matter of seconds.

Toward that end, we draw attention to a proof-of-concept initiative undertaken recently by researchers at Accenture's Institute for High Performance Business in conjunction with the software firm Parity.[75] Accenture and Parity developed a math-based tool for converting real-time interaction data into a time-lapse representation—a network movie. This tool has been used to model the experience of an unsuccessful postmerger integration. A series of network analyses, representing interactions sampled over time, is strung together like frames in a motion picture. What's revealed is a dynamic network that changes shape as interactions between individuals ebb and flow. In this particular movie, the interactions of greatest interest are those that involve key individuals in the (larger) acquiring company and the (smaller) acquisition. Along the bottom of the screen is a running graph of sales of the smaller firm's products through the acquiring firm's channels. The network visualization and the graph are time-synchronized, so it's possible to look for correlations between organizational integration and sales volume.

Although it is an early rendering, the prototype strongly suggests that visualization could result in a new generation of leading indicators precisely because a motion picture can help observers detect early warnings of an impending disaster. By making visible the fact that ties between important people—in this case, between the champion for the acquisition and the founder of the acquired company—were beginning to fade and were not being replaced by other ties, the network visualization foretold serious problems in the months following the acquisition. Three-fourths of the executives and managers who viewed this network movie interpreted the sequence of events as a failed postmerger integration even though the only introduction they were given to the movie was that the clusters represented different organizations.

It is not easy to predict how quickly visual approaches will catch on. For many managers, it takes some effort to see the patterns in a network diagram or to judge a change of significance. In that respect, we are roughly at the same point we were at with ultrasound imaging ten or fifteen years ago, when only the radiologist or ultrasound technician could see the fetus in the grainy black-and-white photograph. Now, however, the quality of images is rapidly improving and prospective parents are better educated on what to look for. We expect that the archetypes we depicted in the first chapter—customized and routinized—will likewise become far more recognizable. And as we grow more familiar with patterns of interaction and how they change, our archetypes will increase in number and utility.

Emotion: Feeling Organizations

In terms of assessing emotion, or feelings, such as energy and enthusiasm, a network perspective and tools such as ONA make tractable a set of interactions that executives have had little ability to visualize and influence. Innovation and energy are unquestionably related. Pick up any article about innovation, and energy—passion for goals, executive commitment, engaged teams, focus and effort to overcome obstacles, and even the kind of nurturing associated with parenting—will figure prominently.[76] Yet although energy waxes and wanes over the course of a project, it has a consistent impact on how and whether people seek information and learn from their colleagues. All phases of an innovation require new information, perspectives, or expertise.[77] Our research shows that throughout the process, energy that is created or depleted has a substantial impact on what is learned and from whom. People are much more likely to seek information and learn from energizers than from de-energizers.

Leaders can use ONA to make energizing interactions visible and thereby take a unique pulse of the organization. For example, ONA can identify who is central in the energy network, allowing leaders to learn more about the energy dynamic so that they can replicate it elsewhere. It can also highlight a key energizer who was previously invisible, and help leaders connect peripheral players to the energy network.

Of course, we can apply the network perspective to the dark side of energy to reveal de-energizing interactions that can damage an entire group or to identify certain spots where energy is flagging and thus innovation is unlikely to occur. By highlighting the key project nodes in the network, leaders can determine which efforts have energy behind them and which do not. For example, Eli Lilly has set a goal to become the "part-ner of choice" for biotechnology companies with promising innovations. At any time, Lilly may have three to four hundred active partnerships of various sizes. Recognizing that poor rela-tionships undermine scientific advances, the company's alli-ance management center uses a wide variety of diagnostics and training—including an annual relationship physical—to help its drug development teams work effectively with outsiders. Going forward, the company plans to analyze its development project's energy networks in order to improve even further its ability to manage cross-boundary teams.

Every person in an organization connects to the energy network, but when it comes to innovation, some play a more important role than others. Knowing the network's high lever-age points for innovation—the points at which a small improve-ment in energy can make a dramatic difference—will enable executives to focus on helping energizers recharge when their own stores of enthusiasm run low.

Design: Building Organizations

The network perspective could trigger new approaches to orga-nization design at a time when environmental and competitive conditions seem to be exhausting conventional wisdom. For example, the redesign of organizations to become more capable of change and innovation while improving operating efficiencies has become an urgent priority for leaders of companies all over the world. For established organizations, especially multinational enterprises, the challenge is to be global and local simultane-ously. Not surprisingly, principles of organization design derived from a more stable world where boundaries between industries and companies were clearly defined and relatively predictable are being stretched beyond their limits in the connected world emerging around us.

Equally important, the newest generation of multinational enterprises—those springing up from developing economies—are eager to avoid incurring the costs and headaches of traditional organizational overhead (such as centralized headquarters and massive administrative hierarchies). These companies have grown up in a digital age with an assumption of connectivity that calls into question the relevance of conventional notions of "span of control" and "chain of command." The principles in which many of us were schooled may not be wrong, but many of them are certainly inappropriate for the issues that businesses need to address now.

So, where does a network perspective fit in? Combined with three principles drawn from physics and biology, it could form the foundation for a very different approach to organization design.

The first principle, *permeable boundaries*, suggests that a system that wishes to innovate and evolve must be engaged in an ongoing exchange with its environment.[78] This principle applies to systems on any scale—individuals, species, complex ecosystems, and even human societies. A species, for instance, produces healthier variants when members exchange genes.

Current examples of permeable boundaries in business abound. Most relevant are instances in which organizations break down the barriers that separate functions, product groups, and businesses in order to stimulate the sharing of best practices. In an effort to shave precious weeks and months off their time-to-market, companies such as Hewlett-Packard, Honda, Johnson and Johnson, and Sony routinely assemble cross-functional teams with clear charters but small budgets—forcing them, in effect, to find ways to uncover and share resources that might otherwise have been "owned" by one group. Other firms, such as Toyota, Dell, and Wal-Mart, create symbiotic relationships with their suppliers—to such an extent that vendors literally move in for the life of their contracts. And companies such as BMW,

Philips, and Merck engage in intellectual exchanges with universities and technical institutes to stimulate their own product development and R&D efforts.

The second principle is *minimal critical rules*, which posits that as systems evolve to a higher order, they learn new and better rules but shed an earlier rule for each rule they add. Chris Langton, with the Santa Fe Institute, one of the principal centers for the study of complex self-adaptive organisms, found through experiments with computer programs that very few rules are required to produce complex, highly ordered behavior. In fact, he found that if the number of rules was increased beyond the few vital ones, the system went into disorder.[79]

Systems with too many rules can fall into Catch-22 situations. The stated rules begin to contradict one another, so people ignore them and develop so-called unwritten rules, which cannot easily be examined and therefore cannot easily be changed. As a result, the system as a whole cannot be improved. So it seems desirable to have only a few important and explicitly understood rules, which are aligned with the organization's values and tacit norms.

The principles of permeable boundaries and minimal critical rules lead to a third principle: *flexible resources*. The number of possible connections available to an individual, a group, or an organization influences the ability to innovate through new combinations. If an organism, for example, does not have sufficient variety in its own resources, it must be part of a larger ecosystem in which boundaries are permeable. The principle of flexible resources is demonstrated in several organizations recognized for innovativeness and flexibility. For example, personnel in 3M move back and forth between career paths, thereby increasing the variety in their skills. Honda has built flexibility into its resource-allocation processes in many ways: how it deploys people in project teams, the approach it has taken to designing the platform of its largest-selling car (the Accord), and even the machinery and equipment it uses to manufacture automobiles.

A network perspective on organization design would leverage these three principles to great benefit. As we've demonstrated throughout this book, social networks and allied forms (such as communities of practice) help ensure that large and often distributed groups collaborate in ways that increase the number and variety of innovations, enable the group's participants to share scarce resources, and align different functions, geographies, and hierarchical levels in the pursuit of shared strategic objectives. Although recognized in theory as a vital part of organization design, networks have heretofore been difficult to see, much less to design and manage. However, with the maturation of ONA, new organizations will be created through germination—seeding new networks or linking existing ones—rather than by replicating known but inappropriate structures. They will build on now-visible relationships between key members of a network. There is also the potential to avoid excess cost and disruption by creating more effective horizontal, temporary, and virtual connections within organizations instead of reorganizing. In line with arguments we made earlier about value chains, a visual approach would make it possible to more effectively design and evaluate alternative models of value creation, such as value shops and networks.[80]

Cognition: Thinking Organizations

Theorists have long debated whether it makes sense to attribute cognitive capability to organizations—in effect, to ascribe to organizations the ability to think. James March and Herbert Simon, pioneers in this field, swung between assigning organizations a limited "information process ability"—meaning that organizations (specifically, top management) can concentrate on a small number of topics or objectives at one time—and a somewhat less flattering appraisal that decision making in organizations approximates a "garbage can," where both priorities and outcomes in decision making are largely determined by the stream of things going into the can (problems, solutions, decision opportunities, and decision makers).[81] Jay Galbraith, James Thompson, Charles Perrow, and others generated theories of organization based on the amount of effort that goes into handling exceptions to well-understood situations or routines. The more exceptions an organization encounters, the more exception-handlers (managers) it requires; and the more complex the task of analyzing exceptions is, the more differentiated the organization needs to be.[82] Most recently, Karl Weick and others have posited that organizations engage in sense-making routines. People individually or in communities strive to interpret events (including exceptions) and then, through stories and other communication rituals, assimilate events into shared mental maps.[83]

The network perspective offers a new take on the question of whether organizations actually think. This new take is, in many respects, far more expansive and inclusive than much of the earlier work on organizational cognition. Rather than limit the search for an organization brain or cognitive center to the very top of the enterprise—something that many researchers have done by focusing their investigations on top management—the network perspective allows for two possibilities. First, thinking takes place in many different locations and hierarchical levels—in other words, organizations are more appropriately viewed as being composed of intelligences or multiple cognition centers competing for authority and resources with which to enact their plans or ideals. Second, thinking may be a "whole body" phenomenon, located not just in one organ. In other words, organizational intelligence is a distributed phenomenon, a composite of different kinds of cognition acting in concert even without a central controller.

If the content of information exchanges (whether e-mail traffic, instant messaging, file sharing, blog postings, Webinars, or wiki contributions) could be collected and analyzed in real time, with appropriate privacy safeguards in place, it would be possible to watch and listen to the organization as it "talked" about emerging ideas and developments. By tracing themes or memes as they evolve, insights into cognitive processes could be unearthed. For example, do new ideas come about as a result of a mash-up or forced confrontation of old ideas? Do prevailing assumptions come under attack only when faced with counter-evidence, or are new ideas most successful when supported by a quiet insurgency?

For the CEO or agency head, it would be extraordinarily useful to know whether key messages from a major communication or change initiative were permeating the organization—or whether there was signal loss across boundaries, levels, or cultures. It would be equally exciting to know whether (and how) problems encountered in one part of the organization might already be solved in another part. For leaders who see themselves as bumblebees responsible for cross-pollinating the different parts of their organization, the value would be enormous.

The Challenges for Leaders

Organizational leaders face unprecedented challenges. Competitors can pop up from unanticipated quarters. Globalization stretches organizational boundaries and enhances the interdependencies among organizations. New technology dramatically increases both the opportunity for connectivity among people and the demand for slices of people's attention. Workforce populations grow increasingly attenuated by geography, culture, and age. An ever larger share of value in developed economies is accounted for by intangible assets, especially the relationships and interactions that spark new products, services, and experiences. It seems at times as though the shape of everything is continuously changing.

However, in their efforts to align, execute, and adapt, leaders can leverage new tools, such as ONA, and a network perspective more generally to address those challenges creatively. By better understanding who knows what, who knows who, and who knows how, leaders can link strategy and structure in creative ways and with unprecedented speed. Rather than finding themselves straitjacketed by a structure built to fulfill a strategy long since abandoned, leaders will be able to craft strategies and rapidly execute them through uniquely configured networks of expertise. Those networks will in turn increase the odds that truly new strategy will see the light of day.

About the Authors

Rob Cross (http://www.robcross.org) is associate professor of management at the University of Virginia's McIntire School of Commerce and research director of The Network Roundtable. As both educator and consultant, he has worked with a wide range of well-known companies and government agencies in applying network concepts to critical business issues. He is coauthor, with Andrew Parker, of *The Hidden Power of Social Networks: Understanding How Work Really Gets Done in Organizations*, published in 2004. Cross's work on social networks has also been published repeatedly in such venues as *Harvard Business Review, Sloan Management Review, California Management Review, Organizational Dynamics, McKinsey Quarterly*, and *Academy of Management Executive*. His research has also been profiled in the *Wall Street Journal, The Financial Times, Investor's Business Daily, Fortune, BusinessWeek, Fast Company, CIO*, and many other publications. Cross speaks, consults, and conducts executive education both domestically and internationally. He lives in Charlottesville, Virginia, where he enjoys spending time with his wife and two children.

Robert J. Thomas leads Accenture's Institute for High Performance Business, a think-and-act tank dedicated to understanding how some companies become and stay high performers. He is also the John R. Galvin Visiting Professor of Leadership at the Fletcher School of Law and Diplomacy at Tufts University. His

2002 book *Geeks and Geezers*, coauthored with Warren Bennis, established him as one of the preeminent writers on leadership in a digital economy. His two most recent books, *Crucibles of Leadership* and *The Talent Powered Organization* (the latter coauthored with Peter Cheese and Elizabeth Craig), pioneer new approaches to leader development and talent management. Thomas has won awards for breakthrough thinking from the *Journal of Management Inquiry*, the *Journal of Intellectual Capital*, and the Society for the Study of Social Problems. He lives in Brookline, Massachusetts, with his wife, daughter, cat, and four turtles.

Notes

1. N. Tichy and C. Fombrun, "Network Analysis in Organizational Settings," *Human Relations*, 1979, *32*, 923–956. N. Nohria, "Is a Network Perspective a Useful Way of Studying Organizations?" in N. Nohria and R. G. Eccles (eds.), *Networks in Organizations: Structure, Form, and Action* (Boston: Harvard Business School Press, 1992).
2. J. L. Moreno, *Who Shall Survive?* (Washington, D.C.: Nervous and Mental Disease Publishing, 1934).
3. S. Wasserman and K. Faust, *Social Network Analysis: Methods and Applications* (N.Y.: Cambridge University Press, 1994).
4. We have distilled these three performance areas from the work of two of the most important writers on contemporary leadership: Peter Drucker and Warren Bennis. Drucker, in his classic book *The Effective Executive* (New York: HarperCollins, 2002), and Bennis, in *On Becoming a Leader* (Boston: Perseus, 2003), challenge leaders to think of themselves as architects (alignment) with a responsibility to craft their organizations into the proper shape for the competitive environment in which they find themselves, as well as the more familiar roles of change agent (execution) and steward of the organization's long-term objectives (adaptation). A parallel argument is made in J. P. Kotter, *The General Managers* (New York: Free Press, 1986). See also recent works on the role of leaders in achieving and sustaining high performance, for example, R. J. Thomas, F. Harburg, and A. Dutra, "Leadership: How to Create a Culture of High Performance," *Outlook*, January 2007. Available at http://www.accenture.com/NR/

rdonlyres/3F0FC8D5-0029-4AA9-A0B3-5F5508F97ECE/0/
OutlookPDF_Jan07_Leadership_02.pdf

5. "The Leadership Debate with Henry Mintzberg: Community-ship Is the Answer," *Financial Times*, October 23, 2006. Available at http://www.i-open.org/Resources/CommunityShip

6. See, for example, the classic works of M. Dalton, *Men Who Manage* (New York: Wiley, 1959), and W. F. Whyte, *Men at Work* (Homewood, Ill.: Dorsey Press, 1961), as well as the more contemporary study by P. Scott-Morgan, *The Unwritten Rules of the Game* (New York: McGraw-Hill, 1994).

7. R. J. Thomas, "Harrah's Entertainment: Instilling a Customer-Focused Mindset" (Boston: Accenture Institute for High Performance Business, October 2005).

8. J. Badrtalei and D. L. Bates, "Effect of Organizational Cultures on Mergers and Acquisitions: The Case of DaimlerChrysler," *International Journal of Management*, 2007, *24*(2), 303; R. J. Thomas, "Irreconcilable Differences," *Outlook*, Winter 2000, 29–35.

9. This point is made forcefully in Thomas's case studies on the politics of technological change in industry; see R. J. Thomas, *What Machines Can't Do* (Berkeley and Los Angeles: University of California Press, 1996).

10. R. Quinn, *Beyond Rational Management* (San Francisco: Jossey-Bass, 1988).

11. S. Denning, *The Leader's Guide to Storytelling: Mastering the Art and Discipline of Business Narrative* (San Francisco: Jossey-Bass, 2005).

12. R. K. Merton, *Social Theory and Social Structure* (New York: Free Press, 1968).

13. N. Ashkenazy, L. Broadfoot, and S. Falkus, "Questionnaire Measures of Organizational Culture," in N. Ashkenazy, C. Wilderom, and M. Peterson (eds.), *Handbook of Organizational Culture and Climate* (Thousand Oaks, Calif.: Sage, 2000); G. Hofstede, B. Neuijen, D. Daval Ohayv, and G. Sanders, "Measuring Organizational Cultures: A Qualitative and Quantitative Study Across Twenty Cases," *Administrative Science Quarterly*, 1990, *35*, 286–316.

14. J. Martin and P. Frost, "The Organizational Culture War Games: A Struggle for Intellectual Dominance," in S. R. Clegg, C. Hardy, and W. Nord (eds.), *Handbook of Organization Studies* (London: Sage, 1996).

15. A. B. Hargadon, *How Breakthroughs Happen: The Surprising Truth About How Companies Innovate* (Cambridge, Mass.: Harvard Business School Press, 2003); T. P. Hughes, *Networks of Power* (Baltimore, Md.: Johns Hopkins University Press, 1983); T. P. Hughes, *American Genesis: A Century of Invention and Technological Enthusiasm, 1870–1890* (New York: Viking Press, 1989).

16. G. Basalla, *The Evolution of Technology* (New York: Cambridge University Press, 1988); W. E. Bijker, *Of Bicycles, Brakelites, and Bulbs: Toward a Theory of Sociotechnical Change* (Cambridge, Mass.: MIT Press, 1995); T. P. Hughes, *American Genesis: A Century of Invention and Technological Enthusiasm, 1870–1890* (New York: Viking Press, 1989); F. Kodama, *Emerging Patterns of Innovation: Sources of Japan's Technological Edge* (Boston: Harvard Business School Press, 1991).

17. For some time, scholars have drawn attention to the way in which existing skills and knowledge affect an organization's ability to recognize, assimilate, and take action on key information by using such terms as *absorptive capacity, competency traps, path dependence,* and *collective cognition.* Network analysis allows a manager to see exactly what knowledge is disproportionately important.

18. Innovaro, "Out-sourcing vs. Off-shoring—The Shifting Balance for R&D," Innovation Briefing 05-05 (London: Innovaro, May 2005).

19. P. Engardio and B. Einhorn (with others), "Outsourcing Innovation," *BusinessWeek*, March 21, 2005, pp. 65–67.

20. S. Palmisano, "Innovation: The View from the Top," *BusinessWeek*, April 3, 2006, pp. 110–118.

21. R. Cross and A. Parker, *The Hidden Power of Social Networks: Understanding How Work Really Gets Done in Organizations* (Boston: Harvard Business School Press, 2004).

22. R. Crow, "Institutionalized Competition and Its Effects on Teamwork," *Journal for Quality and Participation*, June 1995, 47.

23. T. Allen, *Managing the Flow of Technology* (Cambridge, Mass.: MIT Press, 1977); W. Baker, *Achieving Success Through Social Capital* (San Francisco: Jossey-Bass, 2000); J.A.C. Baum (ed.), *Companion to Organizations* (Malden, Mass.: Blackwell, 2002); R. Burt, *Structural Holes* (Cambridge, Mass.: Harvard University Press, 1992); M. T. Hansen, "The Search-Transfer Problem: The Role of Weak Ties in Sharing Knowledge Across Organization Subunits," *Administrative Science Quarterly*, 1999, 44, 82–111; B. Uzzi, "Social Structure and Competition in Inter-firm Networks: The Paradox of Embeddedness," *Administrative Science Quarterly*, 1997, 42, 35–67.

24. "The McKinsey Global Survey of Business Executives, July 2005," *McKinsey Quarterly*, Web exclusive, July 2005.

25. This company's name has been disguised at the CEO's request.

26. This company's name has been disguised at the request of management.

27. M. A. Bell, "Leading and Managing in the Virtual Matrix Organization," Gartner Research Report R-22-1959 (Stamford, Conn.: Gartner, Inc., March 11, 2004).

28. W. Dyer, *Team Building: Current Issues and New Alternatives* (Reading, Mass.: Addison-Wesley, 1995); R. Klimoski and R. Jones, "Staffing for Effective Group Decision Making: Key Issues in Matching People and Teams," in R. Guzzu, E. Salas, and Associates, *Team Effectiveness and Decision Making in Organizations* (San Francisco: Jossey-Bass, 1995); C. Larson and F. LaFasto, *Teamwork: What Must Go Right/What Can Go Wrong* (San Francisco: Jossey-Bass, 1989).

29. J. R. Hackman, *Groups That Work (and Those That Don't): Creating Conditions for Effective Teamwork* (San Francisco: Jossey-Bass, 1990); E. Sundstrom, *Supporting Work Team Effectiveness: Best Management Practices for Fostering High Performance* (San Francisco: Jossey-Bass, 1999); P. Goodman, *Designing Effective Work Groups* (San Francisco: Jossey-Bass,

1986); J. Orsburn, L. Moran, E. Musselwhite, and J. Zenger, *Self-Directed Work Teams: The New American Challenge* (New York: Irwin, 1990).

30. A. Donnellon, *Team Talk: Listening Between the Lines to Improve Team Performance* (Boston: HBS Press, 1996); D. Dougherty, "Interpretive Barriers to Successful Product Innovation in Large Firms," *Organization Science*, 1992, 3(2): 179–202; A. Edmondson, "Psychological Safety and Learning Behavior in Work Teams," *Administrative Science Quarterly*, 1998, 44(2), 350–383; P. Senge, *The Fifth Discipline: The Art and Practice of the Learning Organization* (New York: Doubleday Currency, 1990), 198–202.

31. S. Mohrman, S. Cohen, and A. Mohrman, *Designing Team-Based Organizations: New Forms for Knowledge Work* (San Francisco: Jossey-Bass, 1995); J. R. Hackman, *Groups That Work (and Those That Don't): Creating Conditions for Effective Teamwork* (San Francisco: Jossey-Bass, 1990); D. Denison, S. Hart, and J. Kahn, "From Chimneys to Cross-Functional Teams: Developing and Validating a Diagnostic Model," *Academy of Management Journal*, 1996, 39(4), 1005–1023.

32. J. P. Workman Jr., C. Homburg, and O. Jensen, "Intraorganizational Determinants of Key Account Management Effectiveness," *Journal of the Academy of Marketing Science*, 2003, 31(1), 3–21.

33. R. Dawson, *Developing Knowledge-Based Client Relationships: Leadership in Professional Services*, 2nd ed. (Burlington, Mass.: Elsevier Butterworth-Heinemann, 2005).

34. J. Katzenbach and D. Smith, *The Wisdom of Teams: Creating the High-Performance Organization* (New York: HarperBusiness, 1993), pp. 11–19, 98–104; D. Mankin, S. Cohen, and T. Bikson, *Teams and Technology: Fulfilling the Promise of the New Organization* (Boston: Harvard Business School Press, 1996); S. Mohrman, S. Cohen, and A. Mohrman, *Designing Team-Based Organizations: New Forms for Knowledge Work* (San Francisco: Jossey-Bass, 1995), pp. 63, 82–87, 181–185, 231.

35. M. A. Bell, "Leading and Managing in the Virtual Matrix Organization," Gartner Research Report R-22-1959 (Stamford, Conn.: Gartner, Inc., March 11, 2004).

36. For some of the more classic references to this research, see D. Brass, "Being in the Right Place: A Structural Analysis of Individual Influence in an Organization," *Administrative Science Quarterly*, 1984, *29*, 518–539; R. Burt, *Structural Holes* (Cambridge, Mass.: Harvard University Press, 1992); R. Burt, "The Network Structure of Social Capital," in B. Staw and R. Sutton (eds.), *Research in Organizational Behavior* (New York: JAI Press, 2000), pp. 345–423; M. Gargiulo and M. Benassi, "Trapped in Your Own Net? Network Cohesion, Structural Holes, and the Adaptation of Social Capital," *Organization Science*, 2000, *11*(2), 183–196; A. Mehra, M. Kilduff, and D. Brass, "The Social Networks of High and Low Self-Monitors: Implications for Workplace Performance," *Administrative Science Quarterly*, 2001, *46*, 121–146; J. Podolny and J. Baron, "Resources and Relationships: Social Networks and Mobility in the Workplace," *American Sociological Review*, 1997, *62*, 673–693.

37. J. Cummings and R. Cross, "Structural Properties of Work Groups and Their Consequences for Performance," *Social Networks*, 2003, *25*(3), 197–210.

38. J. Lincoln, "Intra- (and Inter-) Organizational Networks," *Research in the Sociology of Organizations*, 1982, *1*, 1–38; D. Brass, "Being in the Right Place: A Structural Analysis of Individual Influence in an Organization," *Administrative Science Quarterly*, 1984, *29*, 518–539; W. Stevenson and M. Gilly, "Information Processing and Problem Solving: The Migration of Problems Through Formal Positions and Network Ties," *Academy of Management Journal*, 1991, *34*, 918–928; R. Cross and J. Cummings, "Tie and Network Correlates of Individual Performance in Knowledge-Intensive Work," *Academy of Management Journal*, 2004, *47*(6), 928–937.

39. M. McPherson, L. Smith-Lovin, and J. M. Cook, "Birds of a Feather: Homophily in Social Networks," *Annual Review of Sociology*, 2001, *27*, 415–444.

40. M. Kilduff, "The Friendship Network as a Decision-Making Resource: Dispositional Moderators of Social Influences on Organizational Choice," *Journal of Personality and Social Psychology*, 1992, *62*, 168–180; A. Mehra, M. Kilduff, and D. Brass, "The Social Networks of High and Low Self-Monitors: Implications for Workplace Performance," *Administrative Science Quarterly*, 2001, *46*, 121–146; T. Casciaro and M. Sousa Lobo, "Competent Jerks, Lovable Fools, and the Formation of Social Networks," *Harvard Business Review*, June 2005, 92–99.

41. A. Hollingshead, "Retrieval Processes in Transactive Memory Systems," *Journal of Personality and Social Psychology*, 1998, *74*(3), 659–671; E. Hutchins, "Organizing Work by Adaptation," *Organization Science*, 1991, *2*(1), 14–29; D. Liang, R. Moreland, and L. Argote, "Group Versus Individual Training and Group Performance: The Mediating Role of Transactive Memory," *Personality Social Psychology Bulletin*, 1995, *21*(4), 384–393; R. Moreland, L. Argote, and R. Krishnan, "Socially Shared Cognition at Work: Transactive Memory and Group Performance," in J. Nye and A. Brower (eds.), *What's Social About Social Cognition* (Thousand Oaks, Calif.: Sage, 1996), pp. 57–85; K. Weick and K. Roberts, "Collective Mind in Organizations: Heedful Interrelating on Flight Decks," *Administrative Science Quarterly*, 1993, *38*, 357–381.

42. R. Cross and L. Prusak, "The People That Make Organizations Stop—or Go," *Harvard Business Review*, 2003, *80*(6), 104–112; C. O'Reilly and K. Roberts, "Information Filtration in Organizations: Three Experiments," *Organizational Behavior and Human Decision Processes*, 1974, *11*, 253–265; L. E. Penley and B. Hawkins, "Studying Interpersonal Communication in Organizations: A Leadership Application," *Academy of Management Journal*, 1985, *28*, 309–326; W. Tsai and

S. Ghoshal, "Social Capital and Value Creation: The Role of Intrafirm Networks," *Academy of Management Journal*, 1998, *41*, 464–476; D. E. Zand, "Trust and Managerial Problem Solving," *Administrative Science Quarterly*, 1972, *17*, 229–239.

43. S. Currall and T. Judge, "Measuring Trust Between Organizational Boundary Role Persons," *Organizational Behavior and Human Decision Processes*, 1995, *64*, 151–170; A. Zaheer, B. McEvily, and V. Perrone, "Exploring the Effects of Interorganizational and Interpersonal Trust on Performance," *Organization Science*, 1998, *9*, 141–159.

44. C. Argyris, *Reasoning, Learning, and Action* (San Francisco: Jossey-Bass, 1982); R. Cross, R. Rice, and A. Parker, "Information Seeking in Social Context: Structural Influences and Receipt of Informational Benefits," *IEEE Transactions*, 2001, *31*(4), 438–448; D. Levin and R. Cross, "The Strength of Weak Ties You Can Trust: The Mediating Role of Trust in Effective Knowledge Transfer," *Management Science*, in press; R. C. Mayer, J. H. Davis, and F. D. Schoorman, "An Integration Model of Organizational Trust," *Academy of Management Review*, 1995, *20*, 709–734.

45. In their article, "An Integrative Model of Organizational Trust," *Academy of Management Review*, 1995, *20*, 709–734, Roger C. Mayer and his colleagues, James H. Davis and F. David Schoorman, identify a third dimension of trustworthiness—integrity, defined as consistently adhering to a set of principles that the truster finds acceptable. Integrity is clearly important in many situations. Parties to a market exchange, colleagues counting on each other to complete certain tasks, or subordinates committing their efforts and career progression to a superior are surely affected by the perceived integrity of others. Yet it is not clear that seeking out a person for information or advice is contingent on that person following a particular set of principles consistently. For example, malevolent integrity—a condition of low benevolence and

high integrity—might apply to situations that are purely competitive, such as two boxers trying to hurt each other but still playing by the rules. It is unlikely, however, that knowledge seekers would distinguish much between someone who is out to harm them and someone who is honest and consistent about intending to harm them.

46. Research has shown that those who are seen as trustworthy sources of knowledge tend to (1) act with discretion, (2) be consistent in word and deed, (3) ensure frequent and rich communication, (4) engage in collaborative communication, and (5) ensure that decisions are fair and transparent. Under organizational factors, we identified two ways to promote interpersonal trust: (6) establish and ensure shared vision and language, and (7) hold people accountable for trust. Under relational factors, there is some overlap with the trustworthy behaviors already mentioned, but we also identified two new behaviors: (8) create personal connections, and (9) give away something of value. Finally, in terms of individual factors, a person's judgment of his or her own abilities also matters, thus self-efficacy is a trust-promoting behavior identified in our interviews that we characterize as (10) disclose your expertise and limitations. L. Abrams, R. Cross, E. Lesser, and D. Levin, "Nurturing Trust in Knowledge-Intensive Work," *Academy of Management Executive*, 2003, *17*(4), 1–13.

47. For some of the more classic references to this research, see D. Brass, "Being in the Right Place: A Structural Analysis of Individual Influence in an Organization," *Administrative Science Quarterly*, 1984, *29*, 518–539; R. Burt, *Structural Holes* (Cambridge, Mass.: Harvard University Press, 1992); R. Burt, "The Network Structure of Social Capital," in B. Staw and R. Sutton (eds.), *Research in Organizational Behavior* (New York: JAI Press, 2000), pp. 345–423; M. Gargiulo and M. Benassi, "Trapped in Your Own Net? Network Cohesion, Structural Holes, and the Adaptation of Social Capital," *Organization Science*, 2000, *11*(2), 183–196; A. Mehra, M. Kilduff, and

D. Brass, "The Social Networks of High and Low Self-Monitors: Implications for Workplace Performance," *Administrative Science Quarterly*, 2001, 46, 121–146; J. Podolny and J. Baron, "Resources and Relationships: Social Networks and Mobility in the Workplace," *American Sociological Review*, 1997, 62, 673–693.

48. J. Lincoln, "Intra- (and Inter-) Organizational Networks," *Research in the Sociology of Organizations*, 1982, 1, 1–38; D. Brass, "Being in the Right Place: A Structural Analysis of Individual Influence in an Organization," *Administrative Science Quarterly*, 1984, 29, 518–539; W. Stevenson and M. Gilly, "Information Processing and Problem Solving: The Migration of Problems Through Formal Positions and Network Ties," *Academy of Management Journal*, 1991, 34, 918–928; R. Cross and J. Cummings, "Tie and Network Correlates of Individual Performance in Knowledge Intensive Work," *Academy of Management Journal*, 2004, 47(6), 928–937.

49. M. McPherson, L. Smith-Lovin, and J. M. Cook, "Birds of a Feather: Homophily in Social Networks," *Annual Review of Sociology*, 2001, 27, 415–444.

50. M. Kilduff, "The Friendship Network as a Decision-Making Resource: Dispositional Moderators of Social Influences on Organizational Choice," *Journal of Personality and Social Psychology*, 1992, 62, 168–180; A. Mehra, M. Kilduff, and D. Brass, "The Social Networks of High and Low Self-Monitors: Implications for Workplace Performance," *Administrative Science Quarterly*, 2001, 46, 121–146; T. Casciaro and M. Sousa Lobo, "Competent Jerks, Lovable Fools, and the Formation of Social Networks," *Harvard Business Review*, June 2005, 92–99.

51. Among the classic research papers supporting this conclusion are R. Burt, *Structural Holes: The Social Structure of Competition* (Cambridge, Mass.: Harvard University Press, 1992); R. Burt, "The Network Structure of Social Capital," in B. Staw and R. Sutton (eds.), *Research in Organizational Behavior*, vol. 22 (Amsterdam: JAI Press, 2000); M. Gargiulo

and M. Benassi, "Trapped in Your Own Net? Network Cohesion, Structural Holes, and the Adaptation of Social Capital," *Organization Science*, 2000, *11*(2), 183–196; A. Mehra, M. Kilduff, and D. Brass, "The Social Networks of High and Low Self-Monitors: Implications for Workplace Performance," *Administrative Science Quarterly*, 2001, *46*, 121–146; J. Podolny and J. Baron, "Resources and Relationships: Social Networks and Mobility in the Workplace," *American Sociological Review*, 1997, *62*, 673–693.

52. R. Cross and J. Cummings, "Tie and Network Correlates of Performance in Knowledge-Intensive Work," *Academy of Management Journal*, 2004, *47*(6), 928–937; P. S. Adler and S. Kwon, "Social Capital: Prospects for a New Concept," *Academy of Management Review*, 2002, *27*, 17–40.

53. M. Gladwell, *The Tipping Point: How Little Things Can Make a Big Difference* (London: Little, Brown, 2000).

54. A popular Web site at the University of Virginia has created a network of all movie coappearances. It can be found at http://www.cs.virginia.edu/oracle should you want to try your luck.

55. R. Cross and J. Cummings, "Tie and Network Correlates of Performance in Knowledge-Intensive Work," *Academy of Management Journal*, 2004, *47*(6), 928–937.

56. D. Brass, "Structural Relationships, Job Characteristics, and Work Satisfaction and Performance," *Administrative Science Quarterly*, 1981, *26*(3), 331–348; R. Burt, *Structural Holes* (Cambridge, Mass.: Harvard University Press, 1992); R. Burt, "The Network Structure of Social Capital," in B. Staw and R. Sutton (eds.), *Research in Organizational Behavior* (New York: JAI Press, 2000), pp. 345–423; M. Gargiulo and M. Benassi, "Trapped in Your Own Net? Network Cohesion, Structural Holes, and the Adaptation of Social Capital," *Organization Science*, 2000, *11*(2), 183–196; J. Podolny and J. Baron, "Resources and Relationships: Social Networks and Mobility in the Workplace," *American*

Sociological Review, 1997, *62*, 673–693; R. T. Sparrowe, R. C. Liden, S. J. Wayne, and M. L. Kraimer, "Social Networks and the Performance of Individuals and Groups," *Academy of Management Journal*, March 2001, *44*(2), 316–325.

57. Harman's story is told in greater detail in W. Bennis and R. J. Thomas, "Crucibles of Leadership," *Harvard Business Review*, 2002, *80*(9), 39–45.

58. D. Krackhardt, "Cognitive Social Structures," *Social Networks*, 1987, *9*(2), 109–134; D. Krackhardt, "Assessing the Political Landscape: Structure, Cognition, and Power in Organizations," *Administrative Science Quarterly*, 1990, *35*, 342–369.

59. The classic reference showing people to be more important sources of information than other repositories is T. Allen, *Managing the Flow of Technology* (Cambridge, Mass.: MIT Press, 1977). Since the publication of that work, research in the situated learning and network traditions has only reinforced how important people are as sources of information. In our own work in more than 120 organizations, we have yet to see a database or other repository of any sort approach the importance of another person as a key source of information to get work done.

60. P. Lazarsfeld and R. Merton, "Friendship as a Social Process: A Substantive and Methodological Analysis," in M. Berger, T. Abel, and C. H. Page (eds.), *Freedom and Control in Modern Society* (New York: Octagon, 1964).

61. Jed Horowitz, "Morgan Stanley Crisis Grows as Top Bankers Leave," Dow Jones Newswires, April 13, 2005. Available online at http://news.fxclub.com/forex/news?action=printda y&day=13&month=4&year=2005&key=3d3a7f887594b81 069442a22b975abc414362ba3

62. R. Nielsen, "Corruption Networks and Implications for Ethical Corruption Reform," *Journal of Business Ethics*, 2003, *42*(2), 125–149.

63. R. J. Thomas, *Crucibles of Leadership: How to Learn from Experience to Become a Great Leader* (Boston: Harvard Business School Press: 2008).

64. U.S. Department of Labor, "Employee Tenure in 2002," Report 02-531; and "Number of Jobs Held, Labor Market Activity, and Earnings Growth Among Younger Baby Boomers—Results from More Than Two Decades of a Longitudinal Survey," Report 02–497. Available at http:// www.bls.gov

65. These numbers are for external hires; internal transfers get up to speed about twice as fast. The entire report, "Mellon Learning Curve Research Study," was published in November 2003 and can be obtained at http://www.mellon. com/pressreleases/2003/pr111203.html

66. This study was based on the Department of Labor's National Longitudinal Survey and uses a representative sample of mostly early-career workers in the United States. D. Dickter, M. Roznowski, and D. A. Harrison, "Temporal Tempering: An Event History Analysis of the Process of Voluntary Turnover," *Journal of Applied Psychology*, 1996, *81*, 705–716.

67. J. Van Maanen and E. Schein, "Toward a Theory of Organizational Socialization," in B. Staw (ed.), *Research in Organizational Behavior*, Vol. 1 (Greenwich, Conn.: JAI Press, 1979), pp. 209–264.

68. E. W. Morrison, "Newcomer Information Seeking: Exploring Types, Modes, Sources, and Outcomes," *Academy of Management Journal*, 1993, 36(3), 557–589.

69. M. Teague, "Whirlpool Young Professionals Network Named 'Young Innovator of the Year' by Western Michigan Business Review," July 16, 2007. Available at http://phx.corporate-ir. net/

70. D. Brady and J. McGregor, "What Works in Women's Networks," *Business Week*, June 18, 2007, pp. 42–51.

71. For example, see S. C. de Janasz, S. E. Sullivan, and V. Whiting, "Mentor Networks and Career Success: Lessons for Turbulent Times," *Academy of Management Executive*, 2003, *17*, 78–82; E. A. Fegenson, "The Mentor Advantage: Perceived Career/Job Experiences of Protégés vs. Non-Protégés," *Journal of Organizational Behavior*, 29(10), 309–320; G. Chao, P. M. Walz, and P. R. Gardner, "Formal and Informal Mentorships: A Comparison on Mentoring Functions and Contrast with Non-Mentored Counterparts," *Personnel Psychology*, 1992, *45*, 619–636.

72. See D. W. DeLong, *Lost Knowledge: Confronting the Threat of an Aging Workforce* (New York: Oxford University Press, 2004).

73. D. L. Leonard and W. C. Swap, *Deep Smarts: How to Cultivate and Transfer Enduring Business Wisdom* (Boston: Harvard Business School Press, 2005).

74. Data could be captured in any of three ways: (a) *active observation*, that is, network analyses that openly survey who's talking to whom, who gets and gives information, who creates and who consumes energy; (b) *passive observation*, or sophisticated tracking of incoming and outgoing communications, as well as tracking of transactions with customers, suppliers, and partners; and (c) *real-time surveys* of employees, customers, and other key stakeholders on topics such as satisfaction, engagement, and the like. All of the results may then be fed into the visual representation of the organization.

75. http://www.accenture.com/Global/Research_and_Insights/ Institute_For_High_Performance_Business/By_Subject/ Innovation/VisualizingVideo.htm

76. Among others, see D. Goleman, R. Boyatzis, and A. McKee, "Primal Leadership: The Hidden Driver of Great Performance," *Harvard Business Review*, 2001, *79*(11), 42–51; L. Belkhir, L. Välikangas, and P. Merlyn, "One CEO's Product Development Motto: Care for Innovations Like Newborns!" *Strategy & Leadership*, 2003, *31*(3), 4–11.

77. F. Johansson, *The Medici Effect* (Boston: Harvard Business School Press, 2004).

78. A. N. Maira and R. J. Thomas, "Organizing on the Edge: Meeting the Demand for Innovation and Efficiency," *Prism*, 1998, 8(3), 5–19.

79. C. Langton, *Artificial Life II: Workshop on Artificial Life*, Santa Fe Institute Studies in the Sciences of Complexity Proceedings (Boulder, Colo: Westview Press, 2003).

80. See J. G. Harris and R. J. Burgman, "Chains, Shops and Networks: The Logic of Organizational Value," research report (Boston: Accenture Institute for High Performance Business, April 2005).

81. J. March and H. Simon, *Organizations* (New York: Wiley, 1958); M. D. Cohen, J. G. March, and J. P. Olsen, "A Garbage Can Model of Organizational Choice," *Administrative Science Quarterly*, 1972, 17(1), 1–25.

82. J. Galbraith, "Organization Design: An Information Processing View," *Interfaces*, 1974, 4(3), 28–36; J. D. Thompson, *Organizations in Action* (New York: McGraw-Hill, 1967); C. Perrow, *Complex Organizations*, 3rd ed. (New York: Random House, 1956).

83. K. Weick, *Making Sense of the Organization* (London: Blackwell, 2000).

Index

A

Accenture, 183
Accord, 188
Adaptation by leaders, 129–130
Apple, 51
Apple iPod, 43–44, 58–59
As Is maps, 100, 103
Assignments, first new hire, 166

B

Bacon, Kevin, 139–140
Bank of America, 163–164
Behaviors: bottleneck, 143–144;
  chameleon's, 155–157; high
  performers' networking, 152–154, 158
Biased learning: avoiding, 146–148, 158;
  network traps with, 138, 150–152
BMW, 187
Bottlenecks: discovering with process
  mapping, 102–103; effect of, 91; hierarchical decision making and, 95–96;
  identifying network, 77–78; solving
  decision-making, 95–99; traps in high
  performers' networks, 138, 141–144
Bragg, Deborah, 15–16
Branson, Richard, 23
Bratt, Benjamin, 139
Bridging: gaps in cultural differences,
  37–38; hierarchies, 148; network connectivity gaps, 76; positions in networks, 139–141; subgroups, 140–141
Brokers. *See* Key brokers
Buddies, 160, 166–167

C

Carrier, 45
Cassidy, John, 44, 46

Cedarwood Pharmaceuticals case study,
  92–99
Central connectors, 170–173
Centrality of roles, 102
Chameleon, 139, 155–157
Chrysler, 23
Ciba-Geigy, 12
Clinton, Bill, 131
Collaboration: assessing economic return
  of, 72–75; bridging distance with, 147,
  148; building team connectivity, 119,
  121–122; costs of, 80–88, 89; creating
  value in corporate, 72; encouraging, 74,
  109–113; finding revenue-producing,
  75–80, 89; fragmentation in, 49–51;
  hierarchical decision making and,
  82–83; improving, 91–92; innovation and support of, 64–66; instilling
  during onboarding, 162–164; network characteristics for increasing,
  19–21; network momentum and, 119,
  125–126; Novartis's use of, 13–15;
  overinclusion and, 92–95; pairing
  high-potential team members, 112;
  reducing error rates in complex,
  100–103; relationships leading to, 119,
  123–125; required for product innovation, 43–46; reward systems and, 111;
  supporting global corporations with,
  69–71; using cultural inventories to
  aid, 24–27
Communication: increasing with cross-
  cultural differences, 33–34; mistakes
  leading to overinclusion, 117–118;
  tracing themes in organizational,
  190–191
Communities of Practice, 69, 70
Conflict resolution training, 99